The Robe

Frost

Review

no. 33, 2024

CLEMSON
UNIVERSITY
PRESS

The Robert Frost Review is published by Clemson University Press. All contents © Clemson University. All rights reserved.

The Robert Frost Review is indexed and annotated in PMLA, EBSCO, and JSTOR, and is a member of the Council of Editors of Learned Journals.

The Robert Frost Review is published each fall of the academic year. An official publication of The Robert Frost Society, the journal solicits manuscripts on all aspects of Robert Frost's life and work (original research, notes, new manuscripts, new readings of poems, and/or memoirs of encounters with the poet, etc.). The editors also seek reflections and notes on teaching Robert Frost's work at all educational levels. Reviews of Frost-related publications, performances, and works of art are also welcomed.

All submissions should be made directly through the journal website at https://tigerprints.clemson.edu/rfr/, where you can also find the style guide, policies, and additional information. Any questions about The *Robert Frost Review* may be directed to robertfrostreview@gmail.com.

Subscription is included as part of membership in The Robert Frost Society. Rates are $50/year and $30/year for seniors and students (domestic and international). Visit the society's website (www.robertfrostsociety.org) for more information and to become a member.

The Robert Frost Review

c/o Clemson University Press

RM Cooper Library

116 Sigma Drive

Clemson, SC 29634

ISSN: 1062–6999

i

CONTENTS

REVIEWS

Editor's Note

Virginia F. Smith
United States Naval Academy

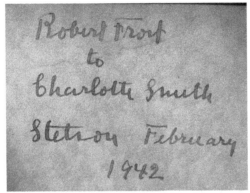

Inscription by Frost to Charlotte Smith, Stetson College, February 1942.
(Courtesy of Virginia Smith)

Today I opened my slightly worn, second-hand first edition of *New Hampshire* and read the words that Frost inscribed there in 1942. Besides thinking about the fact that the book I held in my hands was once held by Frost, I also wondered why the book's previous owner, Charlotte Smith, a Stetson College librarian, asked him to sign the nearly twenty-year-old *New Hampshire* rather than something newer. Perhaps *New Hampshire* was her favorite. If so, I could see why.

Published in 1923, *New Hampshire* was not only the lengthiest of Frost's collections to date, with forty-four poems, but also arguably the heftiest in terms of its impact on modern poetry. *New Hampshire* earned Frost the first of his four Pulitzer Prizes and provided a counter-point to major recent works by other modernist poets, including T.S. Eliot's *The Waste Land* and Wallace Stevens' *Harmonium*. In *New Hampshire*, Frost presents us with the poetic equivalent of a cross-stitch sampler, demonstrating his mastery of a variety of traditional forms applied to contemporary subjects. Sharing space with the words on the pages are the now iconic wood-cut prints of J.J. Lankes, whose images have become so closely associated with Frost. Through the generosity of

1

the Lankes family, one of these images, L.253 "New Hampshire (Apple Tree and Grindstone)," is now the official logo of The Robert Frost Society and, starting with this issue, will be the permanent cover image of *The Robert Frost Review*.

In this issue, we celebrate one hundred years of *New Hampshire* with a special section that begins with a note by Lankes authority and Frost scholar Welford D. Taylor, who describes the prints featured in *New Hampshire* and how they came to be included in the collection. Alexandria Peary, the former poet laureate of New Hampshire, has provided a new preface to her poem celebrating the state, "Deconstructing New England," which we reprint here in full. Karen Kilcup, the 2023 president of the Robert Frost Society, shares her observations on the Frost panel at the May 2023 American Literature Association in Boston as well as original poetry inspired by her reflections on Frost and the pandemic. Classical scholar Nancy Nahra explains the origins of the title poem and discusses the influence of Horace on *New Hampshire*'s only sonnet, "On a Tree Fallen Across the Road." We close the special section with an essay by Marissa Grunes, who examines the influence of Frost's close friend Edward Thomas on the poetry of *New Hampshire*.

We also recognize the achievements of Armen Davoudian and Jonathan Barron, who share the 2023 Lesley Lee Francis Prize for Frost Scholarship. Davoudian's essay, "Robert Frost: Poems in Books, Poems Against Books," was published in *Modern Philology* in May 2023, while Barron's essay "New Hampshire's Secret Modernism: 'For Once, Then, Something,'" appeared in Issue 32 of *The Robert Frost Review*. Finally, we are proud to publish Brian Brodeur's poem, "After Visiting a Former Student in a Psychiatric Unit," which was awarded the 13th Annual Frost Farm Prize for metrical poetry.

Returning author Jim Hurley contributes a note about the friendship and professional relationship between his fellow Iowan, the farmer-poet James Hearst and Robert Frost, to whom Hearst was often compared. We welcome two authors to our pages with their critical essays on Frost: David Raymond examines the role of labor in Frost's poetry and the influence of Thoreau; and Matthew Teorey uses "A Tuft of Flowers" to argue for nature as an inherently disruptive force.

The issue includes four book reviews, beginning with Henry Wise's review of the late Donald Hall's *Old Poets: Reminiscences & Opinions*, which offers first-hand reflections on Frost (and others) by a revered fellow poet. Poet and critic A.M. Juster reviews *Rhyme's Rooms: The Architecture of Poetry,* Brad Leithauser's defense of formal poetry and guide to its methods. John Gatta introduces us to *Robert Frost's Visionary Gift: Mining and Minding the Wonder of Unexpected Supply,* by William Zak, where Zak makes the case for Frost's legacy as an artist and philosopher. Finally, returning author Owen Sholes reviews *American Wildflowers: A Literary Field Guide,* edited by Susan Barba and illustrated by Leanne Shapton. The anthology includes only one Frost poem, but may be of special interest to readers because of its evocation of Mrs. William Starr Dana's *How to Know the Wild Flowers,* a book that was influential in Frost's development as a naturalist. We also provide a select list of titles of recent Frost scholarship.

We end the issue with a tribute to our good friend and Frost scholar Robert Ganz, who passed away last year at the age of ninety-seven. Lesley Lee Francis adds a heartfelt foreword to the family's obituary of this remarkable man, whose personal and professional ties to Robert Frost ran deep.

I close by thanking the talented contributors who entrusted us with their work, the careful readers behind the scenes, our skilled publishing partners at Clemson University Press, and my creative and hard-working associate editor, Steve Knepper.

Jonathan Barron and Armen Davoudian
Share Lesley Lee Francis Prize in Frost Scholarship

Robert Bernard Hass
Penn West University, Edinboro
Executive Director of the Robert Frost Society

Jonathan Barron, co-recipient of the 2023 Lesley Lee Francis Prize in Frost Scholarship. (Courtesy of Jonathan Barron.)

The Robert Frost Society is pleased to announce that Jonathan Barron of the University of Maine and Armen Davoudian of Stanford University have been named cowinners of this year's Lesley Lee Francis Prize in Frost scholarship.

Endowed by Frost Society founder Earl Wilcox in 2020, and named after Robert Frost's granddaughter, this annual prize, judged by a panel of accomplished Frost scholars, rewards the most distinguished Frost scholarship published during the year.

Jonathan Barron's "*New Hampshire's* Secret Modernism: 'For Once, Then, Something'" identifies Robert Frost as a modernist who composed *New Hampshire* (1923) as a groundbreaking response to the pressures of modernity. Though the Frost of *New Hampshire* refused to abandon traditional forms and meters, the great variety of his innovative poems—Horatian satires, Catullian rejoinders, dark meditations, and gothic ghost stories—both responds to and diverges from the more radical aesthetic ruptures in T. S. Eliot's *Waste Land*. Barron argues that in *New Hampshire* Frost pokes fun at high modernism's manifestos and Eliot's pretentiousness (in letters Frost often referred to the *Waste Land* as an "anthology"). By structuring *New Hampshire* with "Notes" and "Grace Notes," Frost parodies the scholarly notes Eliot appended to the *Waste Land*.

Always keenly aware of his competition, Frost, Barron argues, found old ways to be new, offering in the "Grace Notes" "a sonnet's worth of poems" (there are fourteen lyrics in that section) that deliver "a witty and satirical counter to Eliot's then already famous insistence in 'Tradition and the Individual Talent' that literature, and poetry in particular, should be considered a self-enclosed system."

Barron also examines how *New Hampshire* deliberately responds to Eliot and reveals Frost's experimental inclinations through an insightful reading of "For Once, Then, Something," the only poem Frost ever composed in classical hendecasyllables. In Barron's view, the modernistic novelty of "For Once, Then, Something" lies in its opposition to the nineteenth century's "foundational intellectual and artistic premise that a lyric poem must confine its interests to the interiority of a single speaker." By addressing his readers directly in this poem, Frost resists Romanticism's "affective narcissism" by inviting "others" to "side with him against those who mock his own self-reflection."

By directing the poem beyond interiority, Barron asserts, Frost, departing from Emerson, refuses to subordinate the physical world to the ontological primacy of thought and instead recognizes the "otherness" of nature "as having its own independent ontological reality." Frost's lyric poems in *New Hampshire* are novel precisely because they reject the Romantic notion that the human mind makes and shapes the reality it perceives. Indebted to the legacy of American Pragmatism, "For Once, Then, Something" reveals that the mind both shapes and is shaped by external realities. While this idea represents only one of the book's many departures from nineteenth-century lyric practice, Barron uses this singular example to show how all the poems in *New Hampshire* are as equally innovative and original as the high modernists' most famous works.

Armen Davoudian, co-recipient of the 2023 Lesley Lee Francis Prize in Frost Scholarship. (Courtesy of Armen Davoudian.)

Complementing Barron's essay, Armen Davoudian's "Robert Frost: Poems in Books, Poems Against Books," published in *Modern Philology* (120:4, May 2023), similarly investigates Frost's structural deliberations as he fashioned his books. Davoudian begins his thoughtful essay by acknowledging that as Frost shaped and reshaped the poetic sequences of his many editions, he constantly ruminated over the relationship between the autonomous integrity of each poem and the dissolution of that integrity as book collation inevitably coalesces into larger themes and patterns.

Davoudian then poses a central question Frost once asked about his arrangement strategies but refused to answer. In his preface to the poems he chose for Whit Burnett's 1947 anthology *This Is My Best: Over 150 Self-Chosen and Complete Masterpieces, Together with Their Reasons for Their Selections*, Frost openly wonders: "Could anything of larger design . . . be discerned among the apparently lesser designs of the several poems" (498). Although Frost refrains from answering this question, Davoudian states the answer is a definitive "yes," and he devotes the rest of his essay elaborating upon this idea, which undergirds all of Frost's book-making deliberations.

Davoudian locates the origin of Frost's "larger design" in the poet's first publicly performed speech, "A Monument to After-Thought Unveiled," which Frost delivered in 1892 as his Lawrence High School valedictory address. Describing Frost's speech as "a gesture of deferral," Davoudian argues that Frost's address is a strained "attempt to postpone or even avert revelation" and that this reluctance informs Frost's poetry "at every level." Frost's refusal to articulate ossifying pronouncements finds "one of its most fitting vehicles in the poetry book" (500).

According to Davoudian, Frost's early aversion to revelation develops into the poet's famous noncommittal "guardedness," which lies behind "the construction and arrangement of many of Frost's books as well as their dissolution, or derangement into *Collected Poems*" (500).

Davoudian proves his reasonable thesis by presenting excellent structural analyses of Frost's first five books. He clearly demonstrates how Bergson's *Creative Evolution* (1911), with its emphasis on perpetual becoming, informs the poet's thought, and he discloses how Frost's books are never static artifacts but continually evolving texts that mirror the poet's changing thought processes. On the continuum "stretching between what makes a poem radically itself and what makes it like every other poem, each of Frost's books," Davoudian claims, "will catch that different interval that, in turn, will make each book unique" (502). This excellent essay boldly suggests that "like a piece of ice of a hot stove," each book "must ride on its own melting," thus forcing the poet to reconfigure subsequent editions.

In selecting these linked essays as the cowinners of this year's award, the panelists who chose the winning entries universally commended the high quality of Frost scholarship published this year, much of it produced by junior faculty who continue to extend Frost's legacy. As these essays attest, Frost scholarship is alive and well, and Frost's poetry, prose, plays, and letters continue to serve as inexhaustible sources of inspiration that generate new ideas and a better understanding of Frost's place in the American canon.

THE 2023 FROST FARM POETRY PRIZE

Robert Crawford
Director, Frost Farm Poetry

The Trustees of the Robert Frost Farm in Derry, New Hampshire, are pleased to announce that the winner of the 13th Annual Frost Farm Prize for metrical poetry is Brian Brodeur of Richmond, Indiana, for his poem "After Visiting a Former Student in a Psychiatric Unit." The 2023 Frost Farm Prize judge, Alfred Nicol, chose the winning poem from 918 anonymous entries.

Brian Brodeur is the author of four poetry collections, most recently *Some Problems with Autobiography* (2023), which won the 2022 New Criterion Prize. His poems and literary criticism have appeared in *Hopkins Review*, *Los Angeles Review of Books*, *The New Criterion*, and *The Writer's Chronicle*. Brian lives with his wife and daughter in the Whitewater River Valley of southeastern Indiana, where he teaches creative writing and American literature at Indiana University East. Brodeur is "thrilled to be among the poets who have won this prestigious prize, with its prestigious eponym. Frost has been such an abiding, sometimes overbearing, influence. What a pleasure to be even distantly associated with him, and to be invited to the Frost Farm Conference, which I [had] been meaning to attend for years."

Brian Brodeur, winner of the 2023 Frost Farm Poetry Prize. (Courtesy of Brian Brodeur.)

Nicol praised the poem for the "sheer force of its emotional impact" and "flawless use of terza rima." He cited the "hallucinogenic effect of Brodeur's metaphor and the incantatory power of his phrasing." In addition to a cash award of $1,000, Brodeur was the featured reader at the Hyla Brook Reading Series at the Robert Frost Farm in Derry on Friday, August 18, 2023, as part of the 8th Annual Frost Farm Poetry Conference. Nicol also identified three poets for honorable mention (in alphabetical order): Meredith Bergmann,

of Acton, Massachusetts; Len Krisak, of Newton, Massachusetts; and
Richard Smith, of Washington, DC.

AFTER VISITING A FORMER STUDENT IN A PSYCHIATRIC UNIT

I walk the clinic's "Prayer Trail" flower beds
before my drive home. Though my student seemed
marooned by her mood-stabilizer meds,

she smiled (and I smiled back) until she screamed—
the room, she swore, was burning. When Breton
asked Gorky over dinner if he dreamed

in colors, Gorky stared and crunched a crouton.
What did he see, Breton asked, in his oils?
Gorky grabbed an artichoke left on

his plate and said, "You see leaves, I see owls."
I saw my student painting a birdfeeder
she must've made: Q-tips she dabbed in bowls

of pigment, drool strung like a fishing leader
from her mouth held open as her weak neck shook.
I told her once that even the best reader

may find a mirror in an open book.
Others find a window. The class became
too quiet. Most students flashed a vacant look.

She raised a shy hand and I called her name.
Then she said a line I still repeat today:
a window and a mirror are the same.

This morning, her face drained to a chalky gray,
she showed her wrist. She looked a decade older,
her pupils inky as a polished Steinway.

Before he ended it, Gorky grew bolder—
pacing again from house to barn that spring,
a coil of hemp rope hanging from his shoulder.

He wanted his wife to see him struggling.
To stop him, she waved over their youngest daughter:
"Help Daddy—look, he's making you a swing."

—Brian Brodeur

The Hyla Brook Poets' mission is to support and encourage the reading and writing of metrical poetry ("the kind that Frost wrote"). Started in 2008 as a monthly poetry workshop, the Hyla Brook Poets launched the Hyla Brook Reading Series in the Frost Barn in March 2009. The series has featured readings by emerging poets as well as luminaries such as Maxine Kumin, David Ferry, Linda Pastan, Rhina Espaillat, and Sharon Olds. The Frost Farm Prize was introduced in 2010, followed by the inaugural Frost Farm Poetry Conference, in 2015. Entries for the 2025 Frost Farm Poetry Prize will be accepted starting in January 2025, with a contest deadline of March 31. Guidelines and a link to submissions, along with information about the Hyla Brook Poets and the Frost Farm Poetry Conference, can be found at frostfarmpoetry.org/.

New Hampshire at 100
Special feature

NEW HAMPSHIRE
A POEM WITH NOTES
AND GRACE NOTES BY
ROBERT FROST
WITH WOODCUTS
BY J. J. LANKES
PUBLISHED BY
HENRY HOLT
& COMPANY : NEW
YORK : MCMXXIII

"APPLE TREE AND GRINDSTONE": FROM LAST TO FIRST

Welford D. Taylor
University of Richmond

The four woodcut images that J. J. Lankes[1] created for Robert Frost's poetry collection *New Hampshire* represent a decisive segment in the professional and personal connection of the two artists. Although strangers at the time, each had long admired the work of the other in published sources. Therefore, when Frost designated Lankes to illustrate a new poem, "The Star-Splitter," for the September 1923 issue of *Century*, Lankes eagerly complied. Elated by the results of this pairing, Frost in turn recommended to Lincoln MacVeagh, at Henry Holt, that Lankes provide illustrations for *New Hampshire*, scheduled for publication in just three weeks. Again Lankes agreed; though he expressed concern that the time constraint was challenging, given that the frontispiece designs, intended for each the three sections of the volume, must be created from scratch.

Lankes woodcut L.248 New Hampshire Frontis Page. (Public domain image)

15

Lankes was capable of working rapidly (he would occasionally produce a woodcut in a single day), and often under tight deadlines. However, this commission called for meeting—again—the high standard that Frost had come to expect of him, as well as the demands of the poet's primary publisher. But Lankes's determination to please was such that he managed to deliver not three illustrations but four, and it was the fourth, "New Hampshire (Apple Tree and Grindstone)" [L.253],[2] that resonated most strongly with Frost.

In the century following the publication of *New Hampshire*, numerous assessors of the collection have spoken admiringly of its four illustrations, without noting distinctions between "Apple Tree and Grindstone" and the other three. However, the disparities are notable, and two in particular deserve comment. First, Lankes rarely chose the generic technique employed in "Apple Tree and Grindstone." Instead of being cast in his signature "white on black" style—that is, a white (positive) design carved out of a black (negative) ground—this design employs just the opposite: black (positive) images against a white (negative) ground. The application of this approach here is especially notable because of the intricacy of the subject. Lankes was drawn to ancient flora; decrepit oaks, stalky crepe myrtles, and towering elms accentuate his designs. But extraordinary skill and experience were required to produce the gnarled, reticulated limbs and branches of the apple tree in this depiction.

Lankes woodcut L.249 New Hampshire – Notes (Nocturn).

More important than technical differences, however, was Lankes's apparently spontaneous impulse to add this particular design to the three specified ones. The latter group—a farmstead at the base of a foothill; two cedars against a dense but star-pierced sky; a winding, rutted country road—all convey an aura of the generic, rather than a sense of the specific New England context they might be supposed to evoke. Much less do they establish a specific connection to the poems they were designed to enhance. (Frost's assessment—"well enough"—expressed to MacVeagh seems apposite.)

Lankes woodcut L.250 New Hampshire – Grace Notes (Road).

"Apple Tree and Grindstone" derives from a different source: it is inspired, created to honor Frost by means of a subject evoking objects and themes characteristic of his work. Despite the pressured conditions under which it was produced, Lankes answered the self-imposed challenge by bringing to bear his highest conceptual and limning skills. As to the choice of subject, Lankes had recently written to Frost of "the apple tree that arche[d]" over his Buffalo studio and mentioned a scythe hanging from its branches. While this tree, along with the attendant implements (scythe and grindstone) likely served as physical models, a more pertinent inspiration was almost certainly "After Apple-Picking"—the poem that had first drawn Lankes to Frost's work and the one he would attempt to portray graphically at least half a dozen times over three decades.

It is no small irony, therefore, that this fourth design, the most distinctive and technically sophisticated of the lot, is found where it is in the volume. Not only is it relegated to the role of tailpiece; it appears on the (unnumbered) verso of the final numbered page, a position that is all too easy to overlook. This placement has the unintended effect of causing the reader to infer "afterthought" rather than "capstone."

Lankes woodcut L.253 New Hampshire (Apple Tree and Grindstone)

Nevertheless, the image has been subsequently employed more prominently, beginning in 1924 when Holt (as if to atone) placed it prominently on the cover of "Several Short Poems by Robert Frost," the lagniappe folio produced for distribution at Frost's public readings. In the years since it has channeled the essence of Frost, as Lankes perceived it, to the point of being, arguably, the most iconic of the 130-plus Lankes designs deriving from Frost-related subjects. And now it is being accorded the ultimate honor of becoming the permanent signature image for the cover of the *Robert Frost Review*. Both poet and artist would be gratified for, as Frost once put it, here they are, together, "in equal measure."

ENDNOTES

1   Julius John Lankes (1884–1960) adopted the woodcut as his signature métier after finding it difficult to subsist as a painter in his native Buffalo, New York. As the woodcut was not then (1917) a popular genre, and formal instruction was virtually nonexistent, Lankes was largely self-taught in both technique and style. His rapid development in both categories can be traced in the fifty-odd designs that he created in the first ten months. Working mainly on a freelance basis, his creations soon found a place in magazines, newspapers, and volumes of prose and poetry by numerous authors of the period. Robert Frost was attracted to Lankes's work upon seeing "Winter" [L.111] (see note 2) in the January 1922 issue of *The Liberator*. This led to an association of the two, first as author-illustrator, and subsequently to a lifelong personal association. Lankes's oeuvre, consisting of some fourteen hundred designs, is noted for having helped elevate the woodcut from mainly utilitarian applications (such as advertising) to an aesthetic level comparable to that of the etching or the lithograph.

2   The notation "L.—" indicates the number given the designs listed in Lankes's Woodcut Record, which catalogs and annotates all his works in this genre.

Preface to
"Deconstructing New England"

Alexandria Peary
Salem State University

I t's hard to visualize, but a huge portion of woodsy New Hampshire was once deforested for farming on its craggy and unpromising soil, as much as 80 percent, as I mention in "Deconstructing New England." Deforestation is a kind of deconstruction of New Hampshire and my poem a deconstruction of Robert Frost's "Directive."

As a person who spent most of her childhood in Maine, which like New Hampshire is a landscape of cellar holes and rock walls, I noted long stretches of silence between people in a kind of interpersonal winter. Detachment is a choice. Letting go, pulling away, not answering calls, not responding to letters, never inviting people over for dinner— all of it a kind of seasonal disorder. It's a choice to make relationships into landscapes of gaps and absence. In rural New England, it can take a long time to become part of a community. Frost's "Directive" speaks to me because it points to that inability to connect; as he says, "You must not mind a certain coolness from him." In the Buddhist sense that what we reject in others is frequently what we reject in ourselves, I point the finger at myself as well. The girl with the banana curls at the start of the poem is my childhood best friend.

Like Frost's speaker who tells himself to "pull in your ladder road behind you / And put a sign up CLOSED to all but me," retreating further inward only exacerbates the chill of isolation. At the end of "Directive," imagery of coldness abounds; the speaker drinks spring water with a child's toy cup, water that is cold and from a source "Too lofty and original to rage." That's why at the end of "Deconstructing New England" there's a second literary allusion, this one to the end of E. B. White's "Once More to the Lake," where White helps his little son pull on cold wet swim shorts. In my poem, kids are told to go out and play in a winter landscape of rock walls.

But in the spirit of deconstruction, it's a taking apart to rebuild and make something new. Frost's speaker wishes to "Drink and be whole again beyond confusion." I think my speaker wants repentance for their failure to connect with the people around them during their childhood. The thing is, it doesn't matter: nature and life will reassemble regardless whether we're on board with it, as anyone who's ridden on the bike path near the Frost House in Derry, New Hampshire, or traveled anywhere by any means in rural New England will tell you: the trees have grown back, the houses fallen into their cellar holes are neighbors to new home construction, and life continues to scurry and bloom over all in new arrangements of meaning, new affiliations.

Robert Frost's *New Hampshire*, which received the Pulitzer Prize in 1924, speaks to that push-pull inside people to want to connect while facing evidence of a loss of connection, such as the abandoned house in "The Census-Taker" with its door slamming in the wind. Time as well as human folly separates people. For all its New England taciturnity, *New Hampshire* is a remarkably chatty book full of dialogue between pairs and groups, with scenes of community where members are invested in each other's well-being. The poems' many characters seek to share precious experiences, such as a telescope purchased at great cost, or solicit advice about how to live alone and apart. Frost too seems eager to communicate to us, offering advice in meter that just begs to be jotted down on a sticky note.

"DECONSTRUCTING NEW ENGLAND"

By Alexandria Peary

Toss in some wavy lines, an equal sign, and a squiggle,
then a lilac log, boulders with faces, a few phrases
like rock walls, twin marks from wagon wheels on granite.
The tell-tale lilacs give away the cellar hole:
magnetic lilacs, like nineteenth-century girls
in pinafores and blossom sprays, stationed
beside their no-longer houses. They look about to sing.
Banana curls. Purple ribbons tying their waists.
And boulders in the woods act as billboards
interrupted by an enormous Mont Blanc fountain pen,
       lounging
like an alligator. It intrudes. Comes out of my present
time. No. Be less. It's a Bic ballpoint. Bleached by deletion,
"By the middle of the nineteenth century, when de

forestation reached its peak, more than half
of New England's native forests"—according to Robert M.
     Thorson,
Stone by Stone—"as much as 80 percent in the heavily
     settled
parts of southern New England—had been cut down,"
"replaced with 'open space,'" the autumn foliage
is paint-by-number and different tabs throughout
          are half-finished murals
of a single type of tree in a single time of year.
Here's the place where someone w/ a pewter spoon
     kneeled
to plant the Lady's Slippers that still appear,
and the mushrooms like a stack of dinner plates
that run up the side of a rotting tree.
Here's the fallen-in deer stand
and the apple tree among maples making fruit for deer.
Outside the woods, the puff of dust on the road
where the school bus used to stop.
Outside is the failure to stay in touch
or, really, to ever be in touch. I didn't
ever know them (my neighbors) well.
In winter you are handed a white tray
with a few tiny rock walls, short lines drawn with a ruler,
an indent for where a cellar hole could be
a hyperlink to once go once more to the lake
and told to go at it, go play.

"Deconstructing New England" originally appeared in *Control Bird Alt
Delete* (2014, University of Iowa Press) and was awarded the 2014 Iowa
Poetry Prize. The *Robert Frost Review* is grateful for the permission to
reprint it here.

The State of New Hampshire

Karen Kilcup
University of North Carolina, Greensboro

retreat, n. An act of leaving or escaping from a difficult or dangerous situation; a movement away from an attitude, idea, agreement, etc., esp. one that is being challenged or causing difficulties. Also: the action of doing this.
—A place providing shelter or security; a refuge.
—A place providing privacy or seclusion for the purposes of prayer, study, or meditation, or for rest and relaxation; a quiet or secluded dwelling or residence.
—A hiding place.

retreat, v. To cause to move back or withdraw; to pull back . . . esp. when confronted by a superior force.
—To withdraw into a place for safety, seclusion, or privacy. Usually with <u>from</u>, <u>into</u>, <u>to</u>, etc.
—To move, go, or draw back or further away. Also <u>figurative</u>: to withdraw or back down from an attitude, idea, etc., esp. when faced with difficulties or disagreements.

—from *Oxford English Dictionary* online

New Hampshire—both the state and Robert Frost's eponymous book—has been much on my mind lately. That presence has followed me partly because my partner and I are planting this year's garden, carefully remediating our dark soil, clayey and stony by turns, to hopefully lodge Black Beauty and Sart Roloise tomatoes, Leysa peppers, Diva cucumbers, and many others, both heirloom and hybrid. Black Beauty, as its name suggests, is so deep purple it's nearly black. Sart Roloise is bright yellow with purple shoulders, Leysa is fire-engine red and heart-shaped, and Diva is smooth dark green and nearly seedless. New Hampshire is where I (mostly) grew up and now live.

New Hampshire is home, too, to Frost's great poem-book. In 2023 the Frost Society celebrated its hundredth anniversary through a series of conversations on *New Hampshire*, first at January's Modern Language Association Convention in San Francisco, and more recently in Boston at the Society's two panels at the American Literature Association (ALA) Conference. Weaving personal and professional perspectives, my comments here on the ALA gathering—where I chaired our two panels—are part report, part meditation, and part revel in the book's poetry. I hope the presenters will forgive my omissions and misprisions, exacerbated by hieroglyphic notes.

"Its Curves were No False Curves": Beyond New Hampshire

Our first ALA panel, "New Hampshire and Beyond: Robert Frost's Resonances," featured four speakers' reflections. Brian Palmer used "The Wood-Pile" as a springboard to discuss (as his title noted) "The Enduring Presence of Pastoral Verse"; he ranged widely across Frost's work, showing how it reframes Virgil's Arcadia within modern life. "The Wood-Pile" thus represents a "drama of disappearance" that centers the woodcutter and emphasizes the importance of good work.[1]

As Palmer touched upon this poem, I couldn't help but recall my beloved New Hampshire–born grandfather, who resisted using a chainsaw until he was into his sixties. Cutting down trees, he typically combined a two-man crosscut saw, serving as the man at both ends, aided by a very sharp axe. Individual limbs met one of his battery of handsaws. Progress, as you might imagine, was slow but contemplative. Labor coupled, as it does in Frost's work (Palmer reminded listeners) to create an antipastoral and implicitly antisentimental perspective that revises Wordsworth's earlier work but asserts nature's essential role in human life: we need a sense of awe. Concluding, Palmer circled back to Frost's role as a foundation for writers such as Aldo Leopold and Edward Abbey, as well as the Land Ethic Movement.

My extended epigraph gestures toward the word that stood out most in Palmer's presentation and that resurfaced indirectly in other ALA presentations—and has shadowed me since the conference— *retreat*. It resonates, of course, partly because of my life during the past three years. The pandemic propelled my retreat to, and in, New Hampshire. Security, safety—our house in the woods, near a fish-filled river home to otters, wood ducks, and great blue herons—enabled me to refocus, in this privileged refuge, on cooking and gardening. And writing poetry.[2]

Coronavirus Pastoral

Little River, NH, March 2020

Splintered at the base
a supine pine hovers
over the river, trailing
ice tassels. The rush
across rocks
drowns the drone
of cars crossing
the bridge. The sun
splinters through
an old oak, hollow
between big branches
twenty feet above
its mossy base. Behind
the pine, an eddy curls
in a shallow pool
that, come spring,
will harbor trout.

We've learned
in time, the snow
will melt, the trunk
will slide downstream;
unpeopled, the river
will deepen, darken
with a rising tide.[3]

Paradoxically, for me the pandemic retreat meant an advance. I had to
learn how to teach online; I learned how to alter Zoom backgrounds
(another kind of retreat). My environmental studies students relished
my assignments that pressed them outdoors, ironically retreating
from their isolation and entering a different kind of community than
they were accustomed to. Literally and metaphorically moving to new
places. Like Frost, when he moved north.

Frost's own retreat to New Hampshire was, as David Sanders reminded ALA listeners, ambivalent; his relationship with his stern Yankee grandfather William Prescott Frost sent the writer into a place and environment that fostered his creativity. A "dilatory farmer, nighttime poet, and reluctant teacher," Frost composed many of his most famous, and most powerful, poems at his farm in Derry, New Hampshire. Frost, Sanders observed, needed "to withdraw into himself before he [came] to market." In Derry, he understood himself "as a fugitive," living in exile.[4] Sanders's remarks made me wonder whether Frost recognized how his move to the farm also represented a form of privilege.

Far from remote today, the Frost Farm is situated on Rockingham Road, busy NH route 28. Wandering through the house and its connected buildings, one can see where the family stored its wood for the winter, touch the wood stove Elinor cooked on. Steps away from the kitchen, one can smell the animal-scented dust inside the family's restored barn. While my several visits there have been among Frost scholars or participants in public events, they always transport me backward in time and place. Seeing Elinor's stove, I remember the massive, roaring cast-iron Glenwood model that my great-aunt Fan stoked to cook delicate pies and hearty tomato soup laden with heavy cream. Big house, little house, back house, barn: a connected farm in a different sense.[5]

Connections mean people as well as places. Sanders traced Frost's links to the people who inhabited Derry and the poet's writing. Among them was his French Canadian neighbor Napoleon Guay, who becomes Baptiste in "The Axe-Helve," another poem about wood and about relationships. Guay/Baptiste welcomes the poet-speaker into his home, heated by "an over-warmth of kitchen stove"; we learn that "Baptiste knew best why I was where I was."[6] Typically Frostian, the line stretches far beyond the neighbor's kitchen. I wonder: does Baptiste, in the pedagogical encounter with the city-born poet, understand Frost as Sanders describes him (and as Sanders asserts the poet regards himself): a "fugitive"?

Rereading the poem, I'm reminded that in coming to this place (New Hampshire, Baptiste's home), the narrator learns essential lessons about labor, place, and life:

He showed me the lines of a good helve
Were native to the grain before the knife
Expressed them, and its curves were no false curves
Put on it from without. And there its strength lay
For the hard work.[7]

The hard work of retreat, even exile? Of poetry? (Of course.) Sanders suggested that for Frost, returning to New Hampshire meant, ironically, returning to the values of New Hampshire—and to his grandfather's and his family's ancestral homeplace.

What's the color of retreat?

Above the Derry farm, as I envision it in the twentieth century's opening decade, was a sky that was blue, blue, blue, especially the day after a winter storm. (Today's winters are far more likely to be gray and rainy—climate change.)[8] Susan Hays Bussey offered ALA listeners a different perspective on Frost's use of color. Noting that our understanding of "color evolved along with science," Bussey outlined the history of blue, beginning with the accidental discovery of aniline, which became a commercial powerhouse by the mid-nineteenth century. Although Bussey relayed that she could locate no straight line between color science and Frost, she conveyed the complex intellectual and social environment from which Frost's poetry, including that in *New Hampshire*, emerged, and she mapped for listeners the book's chromatic landscape.[9]

I was startled to recognize her finding that *New Hampshire* includes very little color—and that blue appears infrequently, and in only two poem titles, "Fragmentary Blue" and "Blue-Butterfly Day."[10] Gold appears in one: "Nothing Gold Can Stay." According to Bussey, the concept of blue is relatively recent (Homer, for example, does not use the color in *The Odyssey*). If, in Frost, "a taste for blue manifests our desire for . . . heaven" (sorry, the transcription is unreadable), simultaneously, Bussey asserted, heaven does not equal earth but may include it.

Gold, we learned, is the color that "dominates" Frost's spectrum. When we read *New Hampshire*, we find it clusters in one stanza of the title poem, accumulating six of the book's nine examples:

> She has a touch of gold. New Hampshire gold—
> You may have heard of it. I had a farm
> Offered me not long since up Berlin way
> With a mine on it that was worked for gold;
> But not gold in commercial quantities.
> Just enough gold to make the engagement rings
> And marriage rings of those who owned the farm.
> What gold more innocent could one have asked for?[11]

But as I reenter the poem, I'm reminded that gold is a mineral, not a color. It's worth money in large quantities, though here there's only enough to signify love. The concluding question begs for a symbolic interpretation.

Reading Frost's uses of color, Bussey invited us to consider how Frost regarded it as "neither stable nor universal," something "not to be used metaphorically"—an insight that complements Virginia Smith's assessment that the colorblind poet frequently uses color "to express non-color meanings" or uses it literally.[12] Gold as a color resurfaces twice in "Looking for a Sunset Bird in Winter," where it essentially vanishes, as night falls, blue subsides as daytime retreats, and "a piercing little star" emerges.[13]

With some research, I discovered that literal gold in "New Hampshire" is small in quantity and remote in location, north of what is now White Mountain National Forest. Berlin (pronounced "BUR-lin," starting with World War I, as a patriotic gesture) was, when Frost composed the poem, a city built on paper and pulp mills. In the 1920s, the Brown Company (earlier Berlin Mills), the town's leading company, "employed more than 100 scientists and technicians, and it produced hundreds of patents; by decade's end, over 9,000 men worked in its mills, and its assets exceeded $75 million." Many residents today have French Canadian ancestry, reflecting the population that worked on the company's approximately 3 million acres at its height.[14]

Despite much civic pride in the city's affluence, Berlin was not a vacation destination even when it was most affluent and enjoyed train access via the Boston and Maine Railway. Owen Sholes's ALA paper underscores how *New Hampshire* represents the state as unappealing; Frost counters the concept of it as a "tourist attraction." Among the state's other disincentives to visitors was its population of witches, appearing, Sholes observes, in "The Witch of Coös," "The Pauper Witch of Grafton," and elsewhere.[15]

Returning to Frost's title poem, I find that the poet previews these hauntings, averring that the state has "a specimen of everything": "She has one witch—old style. She lives in Colebrook." Helpfully, he provides a footnoted page reference directing readers to "The Witch of Coös" (a later one also points to "The Pauper Witch," who lives near 4,802-foot Mt. Moosilauke). Colebrook is another of New Hampshire's remote northern towns, even farther north than Berlin and only a few miles from the Canadian border. I wonder: in referencing these northern towns, does the poet envision New Hampshire as a retreat? If so, from what or whom? He flees imaginatively from

> The only other witch I ever met [who]
> Was lately at a cut-glass dinner in Boston.
> There were four candles and four people present.
> The witch was young, and beautiful (new style),
> And open-minded. She was free to question
> Her gift for reading letters locked in boxes.
> Why was it so much greater when the boxes
> Were metal than it was when they were wooden.
> It made the world seem so mysterious.[16]

Frost has his wizard's hat on here; who can tell what he means or where he stands? *New Hampshire* is replete with such caginess. The poet advances and retreats, his presence an absence, a mystery. He thus represents the state of New Hampshire (pun intended) as something he simultaneously retreats *from* and retreats *to*.

Sholes suggests that Frost plays on readers' credulity—or perhaps our stereotypes and fantasies. In "A Hillside Thaw," for example, Frost casts the sun as "a wizard" and the moon as a "witch":

> From the high west she makes a gentle cast
> And suddenly, without a jerk or twitch,
> She has her spell on every single lizard.[17]

I conjure the witch as fly-fisher, as lizard-gatherer, perhaps for a boiling pot; the poet (not just "the sun") is the wizard who conjures "Ten million lizards out of snow!"—and admits (boasts slyly, exults) at the end of his magical ability to effect "such a stay!"[18]

Not just witches but "something white" ("For Once, Then, Something"), a dryad ("Paul's Wife"), ghosts ("An Empty Threat," and ghost-leaves in "A Boundless Moment")—all haunt the poems of *New Hampshire*, as well as, Sholes reminds us, the book's predecessors ("Ghost House" in *A Boy's Will*, "Hyla Brook" in *Mountain Interval*) and successors ("Directive" in *Steeple Bush*, "Clear and Colder" in *A Further Range*). Sholes also speaks of how "regional truth" often contravenes realism in Frost's work, and he concludes with two provocations: "How much fantasy can there be before we leave realism and venture into something else?" and "was Robert Frost experimenting with [what we now call] 'magical realism'?"

"STEER STRAIGHT OFF": ALA PANELISTS AMONG THE WILD GRAPES

If Frost recreates the world of New Hampshire or transmogrifies how we see it, such experiments might conjure the definition of "retreat" as "*To withdraw into a place for safety, seclusion, or privacy.*" Participants in our second ALA panel, "Among Wild Grapes: Placing Robert Frost," explored the challenges of locating this mobile poet. Marissa Grunes followed Frost to England—a retreat from Derry—and explored his relationship with Edward Thomas, articulated movingly in his powerful elegy "To E. T." Grunes foregrounded Frost's intimacy with his absent-but-present subject, observing that the poem begins with a corporeal image that evokes Walt Whitman:[19]

> I slumbered with your poems on my breast
> Spread open as I dropped them half-read through
> Like dove wings on a figure on a tomb
> To see, if in a dream they brought of you,
>
> I might not have the chance I missed in life
> Through some delay, and call you to your face
> First soldier, and then poet, and then both,
> Who died a soldier-poet of your race.[20]

Sleep mirrors death; Frost hopes Thomas's poems will haunt him into articulate remembrance. Words unspoken get spoken through absence. He evokes a nearly divine (face-to-face) relationship that transcends mortal boundaries. Thomas's retreat—also an advance into war—necessitates otherworldly, but sadly one-sided, conversation.

Grunes's reference to Whitman, coupled with the language's emotional weight, presses me to revisit Whitman's words. For example, in "Vigil Strange I Kept on the Field One Night," the narrator confesses:

> Vigil strange I kept on the field one night;
> When you my son and comrade dropt at my side that day,
> One look I but gave which your dear eyes return'd with a look
>   I shall never forget,
> One touch of your hand to mine O boy, reach'd up as you lay
>   on the ground
>
> . . . .
>
> Then on the earth partially reclining sat by your side leaning
>   my chin in my hands,
> Passing sweet hours . . .[21]

Whitman has an advantage: he can touch his beloved comrade, while Frost can only imagine doing so. Ironically, given Frost's propensity toward concreteness and corporeal detail, "To E. T." is one of his more abstract poems, emphasizing words such as "Victory," "war," and "foe." The opening line is its most intimate moment, as the speaker-poet seems to be "partially reclining" like Whitman's poet-speaker. "To E. T." is also a confession—regretting leaving something undone that should have been done, unlike Whitman's poet-speaker in another poem: "As I lay with my head in your lap camerado / The confession I made I resume, what I said to you and the open air I resume."[22] Frost's candor, in contrast, is private, even though he published the poem in *New Hampshire*.

Great loss may entail such candor. As Grunes observed, with Thomas's death, "Frost has lost an ideal reader." She focused listeners on the frame poems for "To E. T.": "Dust of Snow," which evokes regret "of a day I had rued," and "Nothing Gold Can Stay," one of Frost's most powerful elegies. "Leaf subsides to leaf." (I hear an echo of "life" here.) "Dawn goes down to day" (and metonymically, "today"). Grunes also illuminated the poetic conversation that the friends enjoyed, referencing their emphasis on "birds of death."

Pairing such poems as Thomas's "Aspens" with Frost's "The Need of Being Versed in Country Things," her presentation sent me to look for the former. Thomas anthropomorphizes his subject, which he locates at a "cross-roads" near a smithy:

> The whisper of the aspens is not drowned,
> And over lightless pane and footless road,
> Empty as sky, with every other sound
> Not ceasing, calls their ghosts from their abode[.][23]

Thomas's poem reminds me of Sholes's emphasis on Frost's ghosts; "lightless" and "footless" evoke his work, perhaps in its stress on absences. ("To E. T." of course speaks *to* a ghost, and we readers just happen to overhear.) But "Aspens," which Frost judges "the loveliest" of all Thomas's poems, ends very differently than "The Need of Being Versed":[24]

> Whatever wind blows, while they and I have leaves
> We cannot other than an aspen be
> That ceaselessly, unreasonably grieves,
> Or so men think who like a different tree.

Such as birches, perhaps? Frost deploys that tree in his eponymous poem as a vehicle for pleasure, for art—"One could do worse than be a swinger of birches."[25] Or, as in "A Young Birch": "It was a thing of beauty and was sent / To live its life out as an ornament."[26]

I bridge Thomas's and Frost's views:

What the Birch Said

> *Earth's the right place for love.*
> —Robert Frost

> Swinging breaks my back.
> Black, yellow, white, silver,
> I come in many colors,
> acknowledge many kin—
> alder, hazel, hornbeam.

My sweet sap rivals maples',
my bark soothes sour stomachs,
my heat cheers cold feet.

I am not yours
to subdue or conquer.
Combing the winter wind,
I long outlive you.
My catkins cast a million seeds—
they make you sneeze and weep.
A pioneer, I feed the forest,
burned or green.
I travel smoothly over water.
Though my roots
are shallow, they split
rock. Unswung,
I bend, not break.[27]

Frost and Thomas reflect on the human-nature relationship, foregrounding trees' affective potential. Yet recent research by forest ecologist Suzanne Simard has taught us that trees have agency: they communicate, nurture their offspring and even competitors, and live communal lives.[28] But here we're talking about art, not nature.

Or are we? Thomas asserts that the aspens are indifferent to human lives; they "must shake their leaves and men may hear but need not listen, more than to my rhymes." Men "cannot other than an aspen be," though both the trees and the speaker "have leaves."[29] In gesturing toward "The Need of Being Versed in Country Things," Grunes distinguished between Thomas and Frost, whose phoebes, swooping through a derelict human home—the remains of which lie everywhere among New Hampshire's woods, granite foundations slowly filling— find "nothing really sad."[30] Ending *New Hampshire* with this poem, Frost closes the door to humans attributing sentiments to more-than-human animals.

Nancy Nahra's ALA presentation kept us among the trees, analyzing a key source for the only sonnet in *New Hampshire*, "On a Tree Fallen Across the Road"—a poem I've often simply passed over. But Nahra encouraged much closer attention; the poem merits full quotation:

On a Tree Fallen Across the Road
(*To hear us talk*)

The tree the tempest with a crash of wood
Throws down in front of us is not to bar
Our passage to our journey's end for good,
But just to ask us who we think we are

Insisting always on our own way so.
She likes to halt us in our runner tracks,
And make us get down in a foot of snow
Debating what to do without an axe.

And yet she knows obstruction is in vain:
We will not be put off the final goal
We have it hidden in us to attain,
Not though we have to seize earth by the pole

And, tired of aimless circling in one place,
Steer straight off after something into space.[31]

As I typed, I noticed (with renewed, redundant awe) how Frost uses meter. Line three of stanza two particularly arrested me with its four stressed syllables in a row: "*make us get down.*" I'm appropriately humbled.

And even more so having learned from Nahra the historical context for the poem's composition: When Frost was working in Ann Arbor, Michigan, he received an invitation from a local Rotary Club in 1905 to write a poem on the subject of "buying and selling." Rotary International is a service-minded organization that, Nahra noted, brings together people from widely different professions, hoping to foster "lasting friendships."[32] I haven't yet figured out precisely how "On a Tree Fallen Across the Road" addresses the club's requested theme, but it does explore the ideas of self-reflection and working together for a communal goal ("to ask us who we think we are / Insisting always on our own way so"). Too, the winter setting—"in a foot of snow"—likely resonated with the northern audience.

Explaining some of Frost's uses of classical rhetoric, Nahra's talk also juxtaposed his poem to Horace's evocative "To a Tree on His Estate," in which the speaker addresses a tree he believes has tried to kill him. Nahra described how "in Roman religion, the calendar was very important; each day had specified activities for success." Trees planted on the wrong day (for Horace, "an unholy day") could "disgrace this valley." Of the planter, he complains (in phrasing that seems darkly hilarious to me),

> That man probably strangled his own father;
> His hearth is probably stained with the blood of a houseguest
> He murdered at midnight; he's probably an expert at poison."[33]

The endings of Frost's and Horace's poems invoke, though differently, another life, potentially after death. And both, Nahra pointed out, conjure the image of the constellation Orion (Horace explicitly, as "Orion the hunter," and Frost implicitly, as the poem veers "off after something in space").

Reflecting further about Frost's "On a Tree Fallen Across the Road," I notice that here's another retreat: literally, from the metonymical sleigh ("runner tracks") but also from the concrete circumstance of the tree across the path, as the poem itself inspires the speaker, and his listeners, to take flight beyond "one place," leaving the lines the poem itself lays down. We might consider, too, that with a Shakespearean sonnet's rhyme scheme, the poem gestures toward love. Not, as in "The Silken Tent," romantic love, but love of inventiveness. Lacking an axe, we have to seek internal "hidden" resources to take flight.

What does the italicized parenthetical preceding the poem—a subtitle of sorts—accomplish? Nahra supplied two implied accompaniments, suggesting that we understand it as "**in order** *to hear us talk*" and "*to hear us talk*, **you'd think we never heard of** . . . ." Is the poem an invitation to join the speaker? A self-qualification, a nudge to regard what follows as a witticism? Both? Extending Nahra's thought to the poem itself, consider: the poem's structure invites interrogation, as the fourth line reads ambiguously. We can understand "But just to ask us who we think we are" as a complete statement, the tree's question to the travelers to contemplate their identity or identities. We could also join it with the next line, which, like the tree itself, brings us up short. Who are we to be so self-centered? We too are part of nature, brought down into deep snow and helpless (at least in a physical sense) to move forward "into space," literal as well as imaginative.

Even as Frost invokes the Shakespearean sonnet, he simultaneously resists following the standard trajectory, combining this form with the Petrarchan model. Thus he turns a corner after the first two quatrains, assuming agency, even mastery: "And yet." The enjambed third quatrain requires we read the concluding couplet as part of the preceding stanza, with the "pole" a turning point that spins us upward and outward. As I read the poem again, I find myself wondering why he presents the tree as female, as "she." Mother Nature is too limited a reading (and too obvious for Frost). A muse that enables flight from earth's gravity (pun intended)?

Virginia Smith's presentation grounded us in a concrete space—New York City—by tracing explicit and implicit references in *New Hampshire*. Like other presenters on our panels, Smith propelled me to return to poems I've neglected. "A Brook in the City" seems slight—as often, in Frost, deceptively so. Frost ponders the conflict between nature and city, memorializing "the brook / That held the house as in an elbow-crook," "the meadow-grass" that's been "cemented down," and "the apple trees . . . sent to hearth-stone flame."[34] The brook itself meets a dark end:

> The brook was thrown
> Deep in a sewer dungeon under stone
> In fetid darkness still to live and run—
> . . . .
> No one would know except for ancient maps
> That such a brook ran water.

The poem is partly an elegy for these destroyed or transformed, hidden elements, but the end takes an even darker turn:

> But I wonder
> If from its being kept forever under
> The thoughts may not have risen that so keep
> This new-built city from both work and sleep.

We could choose to see this conclusion as a Freudian reference to the return of the repressed, but it seems much less clinical to me, hinting at a curse on humans, here as overpowered as the brook itself, represented only obliquely through their "thoughts." The city may be powerful in its way, but nature always assumes final control.

Smith explained how the poem describes an actual waterway, Minetta Creek (also known by Minetta Brook and other names). Researching this essay, I found that the brook has its own elaborate Wikipedia page.[35] I didn't have to delve far into the page's notes to find Charles Haynes Haswell's 1896 volume *Reminiscences of an Octogenarian of the City of New York (1816 to 1860)*, which depicts a hidden history:

> Many primeval streams and water courses existed upon this island of Manhattan. Most of them have been filled up, and their flow checked and diverted; but though not apparent now, they still exist, and except for the area covered by buildings and pavements, with the artificial leading-off of rain and snow water, would appear in their original force. In this year [unclear which one] Minetta stream was fully apparent; and as it was and is of considerable volume, it has been a very important and expensive factor in the construction of foundations along its line, from its main source, near the site of the Union Club, to its discharge in the North River.[36]

Among Manhattan's largest natural waterways, the creek was diverted into a sewer and covered between 1808 and 1828. Today it's memorialized in the one-block-long Minetta Street, which one source notes "is a rare elbow-bend road in Manhattan," a statement that accords with "A Brook in the City."[37] Frost may well have studied the "ancient maps" he references.[38]

As I delved further into the creek's history—a fascinating rabbit hole—I learned more that may have animated Frost's poem and that might underwrite how we perceive it. The city's first Black neighborhood, known as "Little Africa" even into the twentieth century, was founded along the creek's banks during the Dutch colonial era. An 1892 *New York Times* notice announced "Sources of Great Danger: Underground Streams as Breeders of Contagion," asserting that Minetta Creek was historically "a bright and flashing stream," where "flocks of ducks and geese and all manner of wild fowl floated on its surface or pruned themselves in the shadows of the alders that skirted its edge. Pickerel, bass, and pike, the game denizens of the great river, made excursions up its rocky way and lured the youth of the time from chores at home and studies at school."[39] Frost's "thoughts that rise" evoke this concealed past, suggesting that New Yorkers—and perhaps Americans as a whole—will need to deal directly with their futile attempts to control the natural environment.

But given the long historical association of nonwhite Americans with "contagion"—and their consignment to the most marginal land—I wonder whether Frost also references our equally ineffective efforts to suppress the history of chattel slavery. He affirms a strong presence in the poem and stresses his explicit, corporeal interaction with the brook:

> I ask as one who knew the brook, its strength
> And impulse, having dipped a finger length
> And made it leap my knuckle, having tossed
> A flower to try its currents where they crossed.

The three piercing questions that follow seem animated by anger. Linking "an immortal force" with densely caustic diction—"cinder loads dumped down," "a sewer dungeon under stone," "fetid darkness"—packs a wallop. And the "wonder" he expresses as the poem moves toward the end intimates that "being kept forever under" is a fantasy.

Frost enjoyed many links with the city, Smith reminded us. Not only was his publisher Henry Holt located there, not only did he visit friends and give talks, but his daughters Lesley and Irma also studied there, Lesley at Barnard College and Irma at the Art Students' League. Supplementing her talk with fascinating images, Smith took us on a tour of the family's familiar places. We learned how "Maple," which first appeared in the *Yale Review*, traces such connections. The poem also references the blimps that resided at the U.S. Naval Air Station at Rockaway Beach; the largest ones acted as aircraft carriers. Smith concluded by arguing that knowing the background she provided makes "Maple" (and perhaps other poems in *New Hampshire*) less didactic; that as Frost's children's lives started to diverge (no longer "circling in one place"), the book showed him wondering what role he might play in their lives; and that it provided "a way of establishing an entirely new relationship" with them, especially Lesley.

Connecting these diverse presentations as the panel's respondent, Jonathan Barron foregrounded their emphasis on the relationships that circulate in the poems of *New Hampshire*.[40] Noting that Grunes, Nahra, and Smith emphasized places ranging from England and Rome to New York City, he reminded listeners that New Hampshire is both a book and a place, a place reflected plainly in Frost's earlier volume *North of Boston*, "This Book of People." Edward Thomas, Horace, Maple, Frost's children all inhabit the place (in multiple senses) *New Hampshire* explores. "To E. T." expresses a relationship, with the poet conducting an intimate dialogue with Thomas's own poetry, including "his stylistics." While "On a Tree"—unusually for Frost—doesn't stipulate a species, it does depict another kind of relationship. Smith, Barron noted, directs us toward relationships (with his daughters, with places) but also links them with language per se (the discussion in "Maple" about the protagonist's name, for example).

Barron left listeners with conclusions worth further reflection and study. *New Hampshire* is "a book of epistemology, a critique of knowledge." The whole is "a poem with Notes and Grace Notes," of longer poems and lyrics. Persons, places, and poetics are all related. Along with the presentations, his comments elicited a lively discussion that mirrored the energy of the discussion following the first panel. I found myself wanting to ask questions of all the Society's presenters but never finding the right opening. This overview has provided me with a means to ruminate on, and further explore, their vibrant work.

Coda: "A Critic Is Half Writer, Half Reader"[41]

I was so energized by these presentations and discussions that I decided to attend a Friday-morning panel sponsored by the newly founded Society for the Study of American Poetry that asked a question Frost might have viewed with interest and amusement: "What Do Poets Want from Critics?" Organizer Robert Von Hallberg confessed that the title was deliberately playful. The presenters (Elizabeth Arnold, John Beer, and V. Joshua Adams) offered some provocative ideas, including the notion that critics are crucial to understanding and appreciating contemporary poetry (an idea about which Frost would almost certainly have felt ambivalence) (Arnold). Others included advocating a practice of "collective wondering" (Beer) based not in an individual critic but in a collective of critics all responding to the same poet; "imaginative judgment," which incorporates disinterestedness coupled with reader "exertion" (Adams); and attending to the question of what our students want from us—and from poetry (Von Hallberg).[42]

As I listened, I reflected on Frost's potential responses to panelists' assertions and claims. Perhaps he would have appreciated what I found implied in Beer's and Adams's approaches: critical modesty. Adams quoted one of my favorite poet-critics, Randall Jarrell: "The critic . . . reads to criticize; the reader reads to read."[43] Writing humorously and equally cogently in 1958, Jarrell contemplates the fraught relationship his title announces: "Poets, Critics and Readers." I commend this essay to my readers; Jarrell is by turns incisive, evocative, and entertaining. Quotable lines and passages abound, such as "the poem is a love affair between the poet and his subject, and readers come in only later, as witnesses to the wedding."[44]

But what attending this session made me think of—and reading Jarrell reinforced this insight—is that an unmentioned, out-of-sight, dangerous quality that at least some poets, including Frost, want from critics, is pleasure, however perilous that pleasure might be. I'm returning now to Frost's statement about reading poetry that Grunes quoted: "The right reader of a good poem can tell the moment it strikes him that he has taken an immortal wound." Dickinson, whom Frost admired, expressed similarly explosive sentiments.[45] Delight can be painful; it can be intellectual, emotional, or both. For me—and I hope for my students—criticism has become a way of explaining the kinds of pleasure I get from reading a poem, or, for that matter, criticism such as Jarrell's.

Sometimes, as I noted many years ago with "Maple," Frost resists readers'—especially critics'—advances.[46] At other times, we're welcome guests. By turns, Frost advances and retreats from readers. He did so in the flesh when he kept returning to New Hampshire and Vermont throughout his life, and he did so everywhere in his poetry. He offers us ways of moving that remain incomparable. I urge that we continue celebrating his extravagances and the pleasure his work generates, tracking his footsteps across many grounds:

Frost Moves in Darkness

He composes poems the way
he builds a rock wall, starts
with a deep-dug boulder base,

finds the right size stone
for every empty space,
rolls each word until it settles down
between the ones that lay the ground.
His granite lines help keep
meandering meanings in; but play-
fully they sometimes let us leap
inside, joining him to chart
the rows in snowy woods or calf-
filled pasture. Half-
asleep, we hear the phoebes
weep, see flakes sweep.
He makes mazes
of his mended walls, phrases
directives without directions,
tracks the spider's soft conjunctions,
bends birches like parentheses,
spends silver, gold, and green,
staying dawn and clarifying day.
Inebriates cows; harnesses horses
as transportation to another
place. Makes mischief.
Holds hands with elves, strangers,
witches, lovers.

Talks like a woman,
when it suits him.
Like a man,
when it doesn't.[47]

Hearing the diverse, imaginative presentations by ALA panelists, and the rich discussions that followed, has reminded me how much we should be grateful for Frost's resonant retreats—and try to follow him if we can.

WORKS CITED

Barron, Jonathan. Response to panelists, "Among Wild Grapes: Placing Robert Frost." American Literature Association Conference, May 15, 2023.

"Berlin, New Hampshire History." http://berlinhistory.weebly.com/.

Bussey, Susan Hays. "Unmixed Color: Frost's Insights into Blue in *New Hampshire*." American Literature Association Conference, May 15, 2023.

Feeser, Andrea. *Red, White, & Black Make Blue: Indigo in the Fabric of Colonial South Carolina Life*. Athens: University of Georgia Press, 2013.

Frost, Robert. *The Collected Prose of Robert Frost*. Ed. Mark Richardson. Cambridge, MA: Harvard University Press, 2007.

———. *Frost: Collected Poems, Prose, & Plays*. Ed. Richard Poirier and Mark Richardson. New York: Library of America, 1995.

———. *Mountain Interval*. New York: Henry Holt, 1916.

———. *New Hampshire*. New York: Henry Holt, 1923.

———. *You Come Too: Favorite Poems for Readers of All Ages*. 1959; repr. New York: Henry Holt, 1975.

Grunes, Marissa. "New Hampshire and Old Hampshire: Frost's Study in Loss." American Literature Association Conference, May 15, 2023.

Haswell, Charles Haynes. *Reminiscences of an Octogenarian of the City of New York (1816 to 1860)*. New York: Harper & Brothers, 1896.

Higginson. Thomas Wentworth. "Emily Dickinson's Letters," *Atlantic Monthly* (October 1891), https://www.theatlantic.com/magazine/archive/1891/10/emily-dickinsons-letters/306524/.

Horace. "To a Tree on His Estate." *The Odes of Horace*. Trans. David Ferry, 132–35. New York: Macmillan/Farrar, Straus and Giroux, 1997.

Hubka, Thomas C. *Big House, Little House, Back House, Barn: The Connected Farm Buildings of New England*. 1984; repr. Chicago: University of Chicago Press, 2022.

Jarrell, Randall. "Poets, Critics, and Readers." *American Scholar* 28, no. 3 (Summer 1958): 277–92.

Kadinsky, Sergey. *Hidden Waters of New York City: A History and Guide to 101 Forgotten Lakes, Ponds, Creeks, and Streams in the Five Boroughs*. New York: The Countryman Press, 2016.

———. "Minetta Creek's Parks, Manhattan." Hidden Waters Blog: Companion Blog for the Book *Hidden Waters of NY*, https://hiddenwatersblog.wordpress.com/2017/10/30/minetpk/.

Kilcup, Karen. *The Art of Restoration*. North Hampton, NH: Winter Goose Publishing, 2023.

———. "Coronavirus Pastoral." In *COVID Spring: Granite State Pandemic Poems*. Ed. Alexandria Peary, 7–8. Concord, NH: Hobblebush Books, 2020.

———. "Frost Moves in Darkness." *THINK* (Summer/Fall 2022): 45–46.

———. "What the Birch Said." *Stone Poetry Quarterly* 3 (May 2022), https://stonepoetryjournal.com/karen-l-kilcup/.

Kilcup, Karen L. *Robert Frost and Feminine Literary Tradition*. Ann Arbor: University of Michigan Press, 1998.

Kupferschmidt, Kai. *Blue: In Search of Nature's Rarest Color*. New York: The Experiment, 2019.

"Minetta Creek." Wikipedia.

Motion, Andrew. *The Poetry of Edward Thomas*. London: Hogarth Press, 1991.

Nahra, Nancy. "When Fate Places a Roadblock: Reflections on 'On a Tree Fallen Across the Road.'" American Literature Association Conference, May 15, 2023.

Oster, Judith. *Toward Robert Frost: The Reader and the Poet*. Athens: University of Georgia Press, 1991.

Palmer, Brian. "Frost's 'The Wood-Pile' and a Reflection on the Enduring Influence of Pastoral Verse." American Literature Association Conference, May 15, 2023.

Rogers, Barbara Radcliffe. "Berlin: The City That Trees Built: North Country History and Heritage Preserved." *New Hampshire Magazine*, https://www.nhmagazine.com/berlin-the-city-that-trees-built/.

Sanders, David. "Some Ruminations on That 'Plain New Hampshire Farmer.'" American Literature Association Conference, May 15, 2023.

Sholes, Owen. "Fantasy Among the Realism in *New Hampshire*." American Literature Association Conference, May 15, 2023.

Simard, Suzanne. *Finding the Mother Tree: Discovering the Wisdom of the Forest*. New York: Penguin Random House, 2022.

Smith, Virginia. "From Apple Orchards to the Big Apple: The Surprising Presence of New York City in *New Hampshire*." American Literature Association Conference, May 15, 2023.

———. "Two Roads Diverge in a Yellow (?) Wood: Looking for Evidence of Colorblindedness in the Poems of Robert Frost." American Literature Association Conference, Boston, May 25, 2019.

"Sources of Great Danger: Underground Streams as Breeders of Contagion." *New York Times*, January 17, 1892, chrome-extension://efaidnbmnnnibpcajpcglclefindmkaj/https://timesmachine.nytimes.com/timesmachine/1892/01/17/108208486.pdf.

Thomas, Edward. *Collected Poems*. London: Selwyn and Blount, 1920.

Upham-Bornstein, Linda. "Discover Berlin." City of Berlin New Hampshire, https://www.berlinnh.gov/discover-berlin.

Viele, Egbert L. "Sanitary & Topographical Map of the City and Island of New York (1865)," http://www.codex99.com/cartography/images/nyc/viele_lg.jpg.

Whitman, Walt. *Leaves of Grass*. Walt Whitman Archive, https://whitmanarchive.org/published/LG/1891/poems/184.

Endnotes

1   Palmer, "Frost's 'The Wood-Pile.'"
2   Randall Jarrell observes that critics are "mediators" and, as such, "competitors." "Poets, Critics, and Readers," 283. I can scarcely claim to be a competitor, either as a critic or a poet. But Frost's work helps animate my own.
3   Kilcup, "Coronavirus Pastoral," 7–8.
4   Saunders, "Some Ruminations."
5   Hubka, *Big House, Little House, Back House, Barn*.
6   Frost, "The Axe-Helve," in *New Hampshire*, 38.
7   Frost, "The Axe-Helve," 39.
8   Blue is ecologically costly (in many senses) to produce. For example, we rarely see truly blue flowers or fruit because the energy required to generate the color demands a substantial benefit to the plant. See for example Kupferschmidt, *Blue*. Indigo, a prized later resource, generated indigo plantations in the New World that were enmeshed in chattel slavery. See for example Feeser, *Red, White, & Black Make Blue*.

9   Bussey, "Unmixed Color."

10   Frost's collection for children includes blue in several poems, notably in "Blue-berries," "Blue Butterfly Day," and (my favorite in this group) "The Last Word of a Bluebird." It also includes "A Peck of Gold." In Frost, *You Come Too*, 6–9, 37, 52, 51.

11   Frost, "New Hampshire," in *New Hampshire*, 6.

12   Smith, "Two Roads Diverge in a Yellow (?) Wood."

13   Frost, "Looking for a Sunset Bird in Winter," *New Hampshire*, 100.

14   "Berlin, New Hampshire History"; Upham-Bornstein, "Discover Berlin"; Rogers, "Berlin."

15   Sholes, "Fantasy Among the Realism."

16   Frost, "New Hampshire," in *New Hampshire*, 7.

17   Frost, "A Hillside Thaw," in *New Hampshire*, 106.

18   For further discussion of this poem, see Kilcup, *Robert Frost and Feminine Liter-ary Tradition*, 142–43.

19   Grunes, "New Hampshire and Old Hampshire." See my earlier comments on this parallel to Whitman. Kilcup, *Robert Frost and Feminine Literary Tradition*, 184–87.

20   Frost, "To E. T.," in *New Hampshire*, 83.

21   Whitman, "Vigil Strange I Kept on the Field One Night," in *Leaves of Grass*.

22   Whitman, "As I Lay with My Head in Your Lap Camerado," in *Leaves of Grass*.

23   Thomas, "Aspens," in *Collected Poems*, 159.

24   Frost, qtd. in Motion, *The Poetry of Edward Thomas*, 73. Motion compares "As-pens" to Frost's "The Sound of Trees," which he argues evinces "disingenuous wonderment," unlike Thomas's "confidence in his role and ability" 73.

25   Frost, "Birches," in *Mountain Interval*, 40.

26   Frost, "A Young Birch," in *Frost: Collected Poems, Prose, & Plays*, 339.

27   Karen Kilcup, "What the Birch Said," in *The Art of Restoration*, 56.

28   Simard, *Finding the Mother Tree*.

29   Thomas, "Aspens," in *Collected Poems*, 159.

30   Frost, "The Need of Being Versed in Country Things," in *New Hampshire*, 113.

31   Frost, "On a Tree Fallen Across the Road," in *New Hampshire*, 109.

32   Nahra, "When Fate Places a Roadblock."

33   Horace, "To a Tree on His Estate," 132–35.

34   Frost, "A Brook in the City," in *New Hampshire*, 98.

35   "Minetta Creek."

36   Haswell, *Reminiscences*, 14–15.

37   Kadinsky, "Minetta Creek's Parks, Manhattan." See also Kadinsky, *Hidden Waters of New York City*. My discussion relies mostly on this blog and chapter 3 of Kadin-sky's book; see especially 14–20.

38   Kadinsky's blog contains a video showing some of the G. W. Bromley maps from the New York Public Library's Map Division. He shows the years 1879, 1891, 1930, and 1955; the earlier two show the stream's path. The Viele map of New York city from 1874 shows the stream clearly. Viele, "Sanitary & Topographical Map."

39   "Sources of Great Danger: Underground Streams as Breeders of Contagion." The article cites the surveyor-mapmaker Viele, who critiques the city's engineers for failing to recognize that many of the island's streams were not seasonal but perennial.

40   Barron, response to panelists, "Among Wild Grapes: Placing Robert Frost."

41   Jarrell, "Poets, Critics, and Readers," 286.

42 Apart from the chair, Robert Von Hallberg, participants in the panel were Elizabeth Arnold, John Beer, and V. Joshua Adams. "What Do Poets Want from Critics?," American Literature Association Conference, Boston, MA, June 8, 2023. The phrase "imaginative judgment" and the idea of readers having to exert themselves, come from Jarrell, "Poets, Critics, and Readers," 287.

43 Jarrell, "Poets, Critics, and Readers," 279.

44 Jarrell, 290. Here he references readers, not critics, though he acknowledges that critics are also readers.

45 Frost, "The Poetry of Amy Lowell," in *The Collected Prose of Robert Frost*, 88. Dickinson's remark: "If I read a book and it makes my whole body so cold no fire can ever warm me, I know that is poetry. If I feel physically as if the top of my head were taken off, I know that is poetry. These are the only ways I know it. Is there any other way?" Emily Dickinson, qtd. in Higginson, "Emily Dickinson's Letters."

46 Kilcup, *Robert Frost and Feminine Literary Tradition*, 133. Smith's presentation referenced this view, coupling it with Judith Oster's critique of "Maple" in *Toward Robert Frost*, 44–49. Despite Smith's engaging contextualization, I still think the poem is both frustrating and irritating.

47 Kilcup, "Frost Moves in Darkness," 45–46. Tracking Frost is simultaneously irresistible and impossible.

Whose Tree This Is:
Reflections on "On a Tree Fallen Across the Road"

Nancy Nahra
Champlain College

I n this centennial year of *New Hampshire*,[1] Robert Frost reclaims his post as cultural reference point among twentieth-century American poets. His words survive in our clichés: what else to call "the one less traveled by"?[2] Surely no poem challenges "The Road Not Taken" as America's most famously misunderstood poem.[3] Before turning to the poems in *New Hampshire* with its playful eponymous poem, the geographically unlikely origin of that book deserves mention—a beginning found nowhere in New England. The quest for its source leads ultimately to Ann Arbor, Michigan, where the local Rotary Club invited Frost to give their members a speech, on the theme of buying and selling.[4]

A thumbnail description of that service organization proves apposite: Members of the Rotary Club, in keeping with its founders' intentions, represent a variety of careers or professions.[5] For practical reasons, in each club chapter only a very few members may come from any one line of work. In some chapters, especially those beyond major metropolitan areas, that stricture results in one person for each of several trades or professions—which instantly brings to mind the thematized "one each of everything" in "New Hampshire."[6] In response to the invitation, Frost decided (apparently unilaterally) to draft an ironic poem on the proposed theme. That seminal idea, we may suppose, germinated and developed into the poem we know as "New Hampshire" and eventually into the book in which it figures as Frost's longest poem, up to that point.[7]

Frost's impulse to treat a theme ironically finds expression in other poems in *New Hampshire*, too, including the one to be analyzed here, "On a Tree Fallen Across the Road."[8] Not an especially famous poem, it was anthologized infrequently yet notably included in *Come In*, the collection of poems put together by Frost's dear and well-educated friend Louis Untermeyer.[9] The book's material significance, in fairness, merits a brief commercial aside. Simply put, *Come In* probably sold more copies in Frost's lifetime than any other of his books of collected poems. And a final technical distinction belongs to "On a Tree Fallen Across the Road": it is the only sonnet in *New Hampshire*.

An overview of Frost's poem shows a homely subject, straightforwardly expressed in its title, explored in a sophisticated and purposefully structured poem. Its first quatrain counts as figurative. Its four lines evince poetic diction, inverted word order, and elliptical suppression of a relative pronoun in the opening negative assertion. "The tree the tempest with a crash of wood / Throws down in front of us is not to bar . . ."[.][10] As a reinforcing flourish, the second line exploits its enjambment, whose meaning ironically subverts its words about impeding a passage as it succinctly reinforces the central—also infuriating and frustrating—fact of the poem. The second quatrain becomes concrete: it uses "runner" poetically in a perverse pun—to describe being impeded by a roadblock. Via synecdoche, "runner" enriches the trickery as it implies a sleigh, a word that artfully never appears in the poem. In that same second quatrain, after agency is imputed to the tree (now personified as "she"), more word play emerges in "a foot of snow," eliciting the visual image of a human foot—in a foot of snow.

Immobilized physically, with no reference to importuned travel companions, the speaker glides in the next quatrain back to the abstract and metaphysical realm. In a rhetorical gesture of saving face, the poem thwarts any hint of hopelessness or self-pity. Instead, the omniscient speaker pridefully asserts what the tree somehow knows about humankind in the face of nature's wrath: that obstruction is pointless because of human persistence: "We will not be put off the final goal / We have it in us to attain."[11]

Readers familiar with Frost's rhetorical strategies will experience scant surprise at the prosaic formulation "just to ask us who we think we are."[12] Within the constraints of the sonnet's implicit formality, Frost seems to go out of his way to sound colloquial in these fourteen lines. In fact, before the first line he inserts a parenthetical offhand and potentially ambiguous comment: "to hear us talk." We have probably all heard this phrase—but not in a poem. Ordinarily this formulation serves to comment on whatever has just been said, often to inject a quip that subverts its immediate context, as in, "to hear us talk you'd think we never heard of reading poetry for pleasure"! Those same words, before the poem opens, could also be read as ascribing intention to the tree: *in order* to hear us talk. But such incongruities mark only a superficial level of the poet's shenanigans in this poem.

ANOTHER POET, ANOTHER TREE

Robert Frost enjoys the well-earned reputation of being an original thinker: consider, for example, his programmatic efforts to imitate and preserve the cadences and sound of everyday speech—and to do it in poetry.[13] But in the case of this poem, the claim of originality falters. To appreciate the finesse of this sonnet, a reader needs to acknowledge the powerful model or prototype that Frost likely had in mind. That is, a famous Roman poet centuries earlier wrote a well-known poem about a tree that fell and discommoded him too. And, given that Frost's poem first appeared in 1921,[14] it is likely that many readers of *New Hampshire* enjoyed a mild chuckle when they recognized its model, found in Horace, whose poems—because they often extolled civic and other virtues—made him a favorite of schoolmasters.[15] Frost's teachers accepted that judgment, at the very least: the four-year Latin curriculum at Lawrence High School included Horace, usually in the second year.[16]

But for clarity, keep in mind that an energetic movement had already begun, starting in at least 1916, to curtail the study of Latin in American education.[17] It remained true, all the same, that in 1923 many Americans of Frost's generation—high school class of 1892—had taken four years of high school Latin (and often, like Frost, some Greek as well). Overall, though, by 1923 that important change had already begun: the numbers of Latin-literate Americans was shrinking.[18] In his 2019 article, part of the American Classical League's centennial, Jared A. Simard—with his focus on the ACL's 1919 founding—explores its founders' motivations. Situating that earlier year historically, Simard explains that the ACL's creation should be regarded as a response to challenges to traditional models of curriculum—which ordinarily implied classical languages—in American education.

Change was in the air early in the nineteenth century, bringing with it a rethinking of education—stimulated by thoroughgoing reforms to Harvard's undergraduate program, especially while Charles William Elliott served as university president (1869–1909). That interval, as it happened, included the Harvard years of William Prescott Frost Jr.,

Frost's father, as well as Robert's. During his academically brilliant career, W. P. Frost Jr. took courses in classical languages, although not required to do so; Robert Frost, as a high school student had chosen the classical program—following, as he knew, his academically outstanding father's course at Lawrence High School.[19] And when Robert entered Harvard in 1897,[20] he once again showed an academic inclination similar to his father's.[21] The poet, as is well-known, graduated at the top of his high school class.[22] But by the time Frost published *New Hampshire* fewer readers who approached Frost's poetry shared the academic background of their parents. That academic formation, which had enabled generations before 1923 to gauge the depth and breadth of Frost's erudition, could no longer be called the norm. To say nothing of non-Latinized readers a century later.

WHY HORACE?

At least one biographer has noted that Frost's poetry sometimes drew from Horace's.[23] Similarities in tone typically link Horace's *Satires*[24] with the attitude of mild amusement often found in *North of Boston*.[25] In a more comprehensive view of Horace, classicist Helen Bacon notes Frost's subtler but no less certain relationship to the *Odes*.[26] That insightful and pertinent discussion does not include the two poets' meditations on their respective fallen trees in a pair of poems, each of which relies on a measure of self-mocking—Horace's by means of mock rage, and Frost's with a degree of sangfroid that all but strains credibility. Horace without question enjoyed an excellent reputation among his contemporaries. One somewhat unexpected detail of his biography from antiquity inclines a researcher to compare the ancient poet to Robert Frost: in an uncharacteristically personal remark, Horace includes his own warm affection for and gratitude to his father, a comment carefully preserved for centuries.[27] Frost's father died in May 1885 when Frost was eleven[28] and remained a hero in his son's eyes. The high regard for Horace endured at least to Frost's time, as indicated by Paul Shorey, whose edition of *Horace: Odes and Epodes*, available in Frost's boyhood, proved so popular for classroom use that it was reprinted and used for decades afterward.[29] Shorey's Introduction, recommends that students read the poems slowly, "For the Odes are to be assimilated, not merely read through."[30] Latin teachers of Shorey's era intended students to memorize Horatian lines that they hoped to preserve for themselves. Many Horatian lessons endured for centuries, including ones that lasted long enough to be challenged.[31]

By way of example of Horace's lingering presence—and an illustration of the literary competence of Frost's friend and energetic anthologist Louis Untermeyer—consider Untermeyer's erudite satire, *Including Horace*.[32] That entertaining parody demonstrates how thoroughly its creator had assimilated Horace's *Odes*. Untermeyer assumed that his readers knew the Latin poem, an entirely reasonable expectation. *Including Horace* comprises a collection of imitations of a particularly famous Ode of Horace that explores the ramifications of moral integrity. The words "Integer vitae" (a man of integrity) open Horace's poem (Odes, Book I, 22) in praise of upright character; the poem then describes an array of feats (some imagined) that moral strength makes possible. Untermeyer then presents twenty-five versions of Horace's poem, as they would have been expressed by twenty-five different poets—including Robert Frost. In their personal letters, the two friends talk about the enterprise in the way that friends share jokes. Of the version that Untermeyer attributes to him, Frost says: "I have read the way you say I would write Integer Vitae and I promise you I will do my best to write it that way when I write it so as not to make you a liar. Everybody says it's the living breathing image of my idiom. It ought not be hard to live up to. I will bear it in mind."[33] When, in 1963, Untermeyer eventually collected his correspondence with Frost, his comment on his parody of nearly fifty years earlier preserves a playful tone as he lists some poets he had imitated in the book.[34] Untermeyer's rather casual reference to Horace's ode bespeaks his expectation that the poem's fame obviated any explanation or commentary. Likewise for the specificity of "Sabine woods," an allusion to Horace's Sabine farm, familiar to readers of Horace by way of his frequent references to it.

Nevertheless, though astute and learned readers of Horace (as they certainly were), neither Untermeyer nor Frost could have known about interpretations of "Integer Vitae" that later generations might propose: namely, that in the 1970s a classicist would revisit the poem and detect in it an inside joke—for Romans, by way of a critique of Stoicism.[35] Untermeyer's still earlier (1916) parodic book *And Other Poets* shows how far he allowed himself to push the limits of decorum.[36] Only very close friends—with an uncommon level of literary sophistication— could allow and enjoy the familiarity and artificial breeziness in that parodic little book. The many letters that Frost and Untermeyer exchanged over the years provide an engaging account of the evolving complexities of that important friendship, a correspondence that elucidates crucial aspects of twentieth-century American literary art. That the two knew their Horace well cannot be challenged.[37]

HORACE'S TREE

The Horatian poem that Frost's "On a Tree Fallen Across the Road"[38] uses as its model, *Odes*, Book 2, poem 13,[39] is a poem less easily linked to "Integer Vitae," but able to be construed as related to that poem's argument.[40] In terms of comparison, *Odes* 2.13[41] observes its formal requirements as carefully as does Frost's sonnet. Students of Latin find the poem curiously memorable, but not necessarily because it preserves noble sentiments. The ode tells an engaging story; carefully following the movement of thought in Horace's *Ode* II.13 proves constructively suggestive. Horace begins with what sounds like a curse as he fumes against the person who, he imagines, planted the tree that fell and terrified Horace by landing too close to his head. A somewhat similar and relevant omission marks both poems: although a tree figures prominently for Horace as for Frost, in neither poem do we learn what kind of tree. Longer than Frost's poem, Horace's II.13, in a prolonged rant, ultimately succeeds in calming down the furious speaker (presumably Horace), but only after ten exquisite Alcaic strophes.[42]

As the early stanzas clarify, the poet's vehement rage comes from his imagined explanation of why the tree fell. (Frost accepts the natural explanation, a tempest.) Horace's speaker convinces himself that the tree that he says almost killed him was planted on a forbidden day. Roman religion, a civic orthodoxy, prescribed in elaborate detail which days were suitable for which activities—planting crops, opening a business, getting married— and also days when specific acts (including planting a tree) were explicitly forbidden. Apparently satisfied with this fictive root of his troubles, Horace then portrays the kind of man who would have done such a heinous thing. According to Horace, that man's crimes violated taboos: he had probably strangled his own father, murdered a guest, and strewn the victim's innards around the house at midnight. Horace then observes in an avuncular tone that people tend not to be wary of the things they should.

By poem's end the speaker—only slightly less angry and terrified—still thinking his death is imminent, achieves a vision and a version of the underworld of the afterlife. There, moral satisfaction offsets his trauma: in that realm, which Horace insists he almost experienced, poets enjoy ease and prestige. Poets, the ode implies, have less to fear in dying than have other mortals. In a perverse way, such a message counts as less than grim and dreadful, having been mollified apparently by a special dispensation for poets.

POINTS OF COMPARISON

Frost, I am confident, had Horace's ode in mind in some way when he wrote about his New Hampshire tree that had fallen. Frost's sonnet, via its sonnet form, offers a grid on which to take measure of its speaker's strategy. We look for a turn (volta) and we find one.[43] But with Horace in mind, we understand that Frost is updating the ancient model and having some fun doing it. No one dies in Frost's poem, and we cannot easily determine whether anyone is in danger. Context inclines us to do some supposing about what seems implied. The word "sleigh" appears nowhere, but we know there are runners and a reference about getting down (as from a sleigh).

Call it fatalistic or call it optimistic, plainly the conclusion of Frost's poem looks forward to no afterlife in any traditional sense, but its tone sounds hopeful. The poem allows an ironic observation about human optimism: "debating what to do without an ax"[44] points to an urge to insist on the possibility of some version of rescue or, at the very least, of survival. Finally the poem all but cheers human resilience—a word as conspicuously absent as was the sleigh—"[the goal that] . . . we know we have it in us to attain."[45]

If we look for parallels between Frost's sonnet and Horace's ode, subject matter, regard for poetic form, and an optimistic ending for a precarious situation make the two poems align. Their differences prove extensive and instructive. Briefly, the solace that Horace found in imagining a placid afterlife that privileges poets matches the resolution of Frost's speculative conclusion. Frost, unlike Horace, avoids fantastic claims, or at any rate sketches an incomplete but plausible story.

OVERVIEW AND IMPLICATIONS

What matters here cannot, I hope, be called surprising. It is not that Frost wrote a poem on Horace's theme, possibly by coincidence. More to the point, Frost adapted ancient insights into the ethical weight of poetry, which Horace explored in a world rife with superstitions and able to tolerate polytheistic beliefs. Frost saw through or, rather, saw beyond Roman (pre-Enlightenment) limitations to appreciate what Horace valued; he arrived at a New England meditation on being humbled by nature. We now appreciate that Frost's poem, when it attributes agency to a tree, in effect alludes to Horace's world— wherein the concept of nature being indifferent could find neither easy nor wide acceptance. Frost, for his part, held to hope in the idea of taking confident action—after first mocking his own awareness of the impossibility of a practicable solution: "Debating what to do without an ax"—in iambic pentameter. Here he expresses hope by opening up his poem's perspective spatially. Both "seizing earth by the pole" and "Steer[ing] straight off after something into space" (lines 12–14) count as solutions only in an expanded and imagined realm. That recalibration of planetary scale matches the temporal expansion of the poem's perspective, already evinced by the lively assimilation of a kindred *ancient* poet. Very far from New Hampshire indeed.

Reuben Brower recognized Frost's paradigm when he called "New Hampshire" one of Frost's "essay poems," asserting that category to be "impure, [because] composed in a transitional form on the way between the nature monologue and the classic essay poem, the Horatian *sermo.*"[46] At the same time we must allow for an ongoing evolution in the reception of the Frost corpus, as this analysis acknowledges but cannot fully explore here. For this discussion, the vital point about a numerical decline in the teaching of Latin is, quite simply, that it had already begun in Frost's teenage years.[47] A shift in beliefs about the purpose of education, of course, happens ineluctably in the context of a reevaluation of other broad cultural tenets. Poetry, of necessity, likewise feels any seismic shift of that magnitude, while at the same time a change in what the young are taught guarantees a new species of reader. It was exactly at the crux of these massive considerations that poets challenged readers to confront their own cultural milieu. By way of example, moment T. S. Eliot's studiously daunting creation *The Waste Land* appeared in book form in December 1922;[48] less than a year later, on November 3, 1923, Holt published Frost's just as studiously unpretentious *New Hampshire: A Poem with Notes and Grace Notes*.[49] The vertiginous interplay between those two very odd bedfellows continues to invite scholarly inquiry,[50] which affirms a view of that moment's soul-searching writ large. Frost, as forward observer or, better yet as the vanguard (literally *avant garde*) took extra risk being among the first to engage the enemy. With such a moment in mind, we may more readily approach Frost's poem that memorializes a day when a distressed tree sent a discreetly innovative poet back to his poetic roots.

WORKS CITED

Bacon, Helen. "Dialogue of Poets: 'Mens Animi' and the Renewal of Words." *The Massachusetts Review* 19, no. 2 (1978): 319–34.

———. "Frost and the Ancient Muses." In *The Cambridge Companion to Robert Frost*, edited by Robert Faggen, 75–100. Cambridge: Cambridge University Press, 2001.

———. "'In- and Outdoor Schooling': Robert Frost and the Classics." In *Robert Frost: Lectures on the Centennial of His Birth*. Washington, DC: The Library of Congress, 1975.

Brower, Reuben. *The Poetry of Robert Frost: Constellations of Intention*. Oxford: Oxford University Press, 1963.

Cornell, T. J. *The Beginnings of Rome*. London; New York: Routledge, 1995.

Cramer, Jeffrey S. *Robert Frost Among His Poems*. Jefferson, NC: McFarland, 1996.

Crashaw, Richard (1612–1649). Translated Horace *Odes* II.13 into Greek. https://www.gutenberg.org/files/38550/38550-h/38550-h.htm#HORATII_ODE.

"First Four Rotarians, The." Rotary International. https://www.rotary.org/en/history-first-four-rotarians.

Frost, Robert. *Collected Poems, Prose, & Plays* (referred to herein as Frost, *CPPP*), edited by Richard Poirier and Mark Richardson. New York: The Library of America, 1995.

———. *Come In, and Other Poems*. Commentary by Louis Untermeyer. New York: Henry Holt and Company, 1943.

———. *The Letters of Robert Frost, 1 1886–1920* ,edited by Donald Sheehy, Mark Richardson, and Robert Faggen. Cambridge, MA: Harvard University Press, 2014.

———. *The Letters of Robert Frost, 2 1920–1928*, edited by Donald Sheehy, Mark Richardson, Robert Bernard Hass, and Henry Atmore. Cambridge, MA: Harvard University Press, 2016.

———. *The Letters of Robert Frost to Louis Untermeyer*. New York: Holt, Rinehart and Winston, 1963.

Horace (Quintus Horatius Flaccus). *Horace: Odes and Epodes*, edited by Paul Shorey. Revised by Paul Shorey and Gordon J. Laing. Chicago: Sanborn, 1919. The Students' Series of Latin Classics.

———. *The Odes of Horace*. Book 2. Ode 13. Translated by David Ferry, 132–35. New York: Farrar, Straus and Giroux, 1997.

Gaisser, Julia Haig. *Horace. Odes & Epodes*: A New Annotated Latin Edition, edited by Daniel H. Garrison. Norman: University of Oklahoma Press, 1991.

———. *Horace: Satires, Epistles and* Ars Poetica. Translated by H. Rushton Fairclough. Loeb Classical Library. Cambridge, MA: Harvard University Press, 1970.

———. "The Roman Odes at School: The Rise of the Imperial Horace." *The Classical World* 87, no. 5 (1994): 443–56. https://doi.org/10.2307/4351539.

Horace. *Horace in English*, edited by D. A. Carne-Ross and Kenneth Haynes. Odes II.13, translated by Richard Crashaw, 94–96. London: Penguin, 1996.

McCormick, Jane. "Horace's 'Integer Vitae.'" Odes I.22 *The Classical World* 67, no. 1 (1973): 28–33. https://doi.org/10.2307/4347944.

Miller, Christopher Patrick. "A Strangeness in Common: Trespass, Drift, and Extravagance in Robert Frost." *Journal of Modern Literature* 40, no. 2 (Winter 2017): 60–78. doi:https://doi.org/10.2919/jmodelite.40.2.04.

Nahra, Nancy. "'My Kind of Fooling': Robert Frost's 'A Hundred Collars' and North of Boston's *Variations on Horace*." *Robert Frost Review*, no. 23/24 (2013/14): 86–105.

Newlands, Carole. *Playing with Time: Ovid and the Fasti*. Ithaca, NY: Cornell University Press, 1995. Series: Cornell Studies in Classical Philology v.55.

Orr, David. *The Road Not Taken: Finding America in the Poem Everyone Loves and Almost Everyone Gets Wrong*. New York: Penguin, 2015.

Parini, Jay. *Robert Frost: A Life*. New York: Holt, 1999.

Pound, Ezra. "Horace." *Arion: A Journal of Humanities and the Classics* 9, no. 2/3 (1970): 178–87. http://www.jstor.org/stable/20163255.

Simard, Jared A. "Latin Under Siege and the Founding of the ACL." *The Classical Outlook* 95, no. 1 (2020): 9–14.

Suetonius, *Suetonius* Vol. II. *Vita Horati*, translated by J. C. Rolfe, 484–91. Loeb Classical Library "On Poets-Horace." Cambridge: Harvard University Press, 1965.

Thompson, Lawrance. *Robert Frost: The Years of Triumph 1915–1938*. New York: Holt, 1970.

Tomlinson, Charles. "Some Aspects of Horace in the Twentieth Century." In *Horace Made New: Horatian Influences on British Writing from the Renaissance to the Twentieth Century*, edited by Charles Martindale and David Hopkins, 240–257. New York: Cambridge University Press, 1993.

Untermeyer, Louis. *And Other Poets*. New York: Holt, 1916.

———. *Including Horace*. New York: Harcourt, Brace and Howe, 1919. Reprinted Middletown, DE: Bibliobazaar, 2016.

ENDNOTES

1 Frost, CPPP, 150–223.

2 Frost, CPPP, 103.19.

3 Orr, *The Road Not Taken*, 1–17.

4 Thompson, *Years of Triumph, 1915–1938*, 230.

5 "The First Four Rotarians," Rotary International.

6 Frost, CPPP, 152.62.

7 "New Hampshire" with its 413 lines held that distinction until displaced by "Kitty Hawk" (471 lines) in 1962 in *In the Clearing*. For evolving versions of "Kitty Hawk," see Cramer, *Robert Frost Among His Poems*, 167–71.

8 Frost, CPPP, 220.

9 Frost, *The Letters of Robert Frost to Louis Untermeyer*, 351; Cramer, *Robert Frost Among His Poems*, 85.

10 Frost, CPPP, 220.1–2.

11 Frost, CPPP, 220.11.

12 Frost, CPPP, 220.8. See Frost's comment on this poem in 1947: "Most accidents are just to ask us who we think we are. And after all who in Hell are we?" *Letters of Robert Frost to Louis Untermeyer*, 351.

13 Frost, *Letters 1886–1920*, 121–23.

14 In *Farm and Fireside*, October 1921. Cramer (85) notes that in the periodical no parenthetical remark appears after the poem's title.

15 That Horace was a favorite of schoolmasters.

16 Lawrence Historical Society, Lawrence, Massachusetts. School reports detail the courses required in the three available courses: academic, general, and commercial.

17 During his academically brilliant career, W. P. Frost took courses in classical languages, although not required to do so; Robert Frost, after having chosen the classical course in high school—following, as he knew, the choice his father had made at Lawrence High School (Thompson, *Early Years*, 79). The poet, as is well known, graduated at the top of his class.

18 See Simard, "Latin Under Siege."

19 Thompson, *Early Years*, 79.

20 By the time he entered Harvard, Frost had already sampled college life by spending barely three months at Dartmouth before simply going home with no intention of returning and without informing the college, as discussed in Parini, *Robert Frost: A Life*, 34–37. Five years later in September, as a married man with one child Frost again started a college career at Harvard; in March 1899 he withdrew from Harvard having learned that soon he would have a second child. Thompson, *Early Years*, 234–48.

21 Harvard University Archives record that Frost signed up for a sequence of Latin courses that began with Livy. He did not major in classics—or in anything. Majors were not yet the standard practice: President Eliot had revamped the curriculum to encourage students to choose electives freely.

22 Thompson, *Early Years*, 124–25.

23 Parini, *Robert Frost: A Life*, 24.

24 Horace, *Satires*; Loeb xi–xxv.

25 Parini, *Robert Frost: A Life*, 209; see also Nahra, "'My Kind of Fooling,'" 86–105.

26 Bacon, "Ancient Muses," 77–80. See her analysis of "Hyla Brook," alongside Horace's elegant Ode (3.13).

27 Suetonius (Gaius Suetonius Tranquillus 69 CE—after 122 CE). *Lives of the Caesars*, Vol. II. Horace Translated by J. C. Rolfe. Loeb, 1914. See also *Horace: Satires* I.4.

28 Frost, CPPP, 931. See Parini, *Robert Frost: A Life*, 18–20; Thompson, Early Years, 44–45.

29 *Horace: Odes and Epodes*, edited by Paul Shorey, revised by Paul Shorey and Gordon J. Laing. Chicago: Sanborn, 1919. The Students' Series of Latin Classics.

30 Horace, Shorey edition, vi. See also Garrison, Introduction, xii.

31 Famously Dulce et decorum est pro patria mori (Odes Book 3, poem 2.13) [It is a sweet and fitting thing to die for one's home country] did not age well. Wilfred Owen satirically deflates Horace's lofty in his poem that repurposes the Latin words as its title, "Dulce at decorum est." https://www.poetryfoundation.org/poems/46560/dulce-et-decorum-est.

32 As the elliptical title hints, this volume of parodies continues the theme of Untermeyer's earlier parody "And Other Poets" (1916), which frames its imitations at a hypothetical event, "The Banquet of the Bards." That collection includes his friend Robert in "Robert Frost Relates 'The Death of the Tired Man,'" in which the poet parodies the nursery rhyme "Solomon Grundy."

33 Frost, *Letters: 1886–1920*, 641. Frost wrote the letter from Amherst, Massachusetts, on January 4, 1919. He had been quite ill with influenza during the 1918–1919 pandemic. The letter refers to his weakened health.

34 "An occasional translator, I was also a part-time parodist. A volume entitled Including Horace began with a set of paraphrases of the Horatian "Integer Vitae" ode rendered in the manner of twenty-five poets, including Robert Herrick, Robert Browning, Robert Bridges, and Robert Frost. Robert liked the [Edwin Arlington] Robinson pastiche better than my transplanting of the Sabine woods to his own New Hampshire acres." Frost, *Letters to Louis Untermeyer*, 81.

35 Jane McCormick, "Horace's 'Integer Vitae,'" 1973.

36 To frame his virtuoso piece, Untermeyer invents "The Banquet of the Bards," an imagined assemblage of poets, living and dead, who interact by proposing poems that occasionally evoke nursery rhymes. Frost appears in a section entitled "Robert Frost Relates The Death of the Tired Man." Only very close friends—with an uncommon level of literary sophistication—could allow and enjoy that familiarity and artificial breeziness.

37 Bacon, "'In- and Outdoor Schooling,'" 23n1. Frost's "For Once, Then, Something" in *New Hampshire*; "The Lesson for Today" (Frost, CPPP, 318–322) was Horatian. See Tomlinson, *Horace Made New*, 311–12 in 1942 shows Horace's influence early and later in the Frost oeuvre.

38 Frost, CPPP, 220.

39 Horace *The Odes*, Book 2, Ode 13, 132–35.

40 Horace himself, arguably a man of good character, likewise escaped danger, according to the poem whose theme—and much more—Frost imitates in relating his encounter with a fallen tree.

41 Horace *The Odes*, Book 2, Ode 13, 132–35.

42 An appropriate choice thematized in the poem by the presence of the Greek poet Alcaeus, for whom it is named. Greek in origin, Alcaic meter is here adapted to Latin as part of Horace's technical achievement.

43 After line 12, for Shakespearean sonnet form.

44 Frost, CPPP, 220.8.

45 Frost, CPPP, 220.11.

46 Brower, *Poetry: Constellations*, 199–203.

47 Simard, 9–10 and above.

48 Eliot's poem had been published in the British journal *Criterion* in October 1922 and in the magazine the *Dial* in the following month. New York publisher Boni & Liveright published it in book form in December 1922; Hogarth Press in England published it in 1923.

49 Frost, CPPP, 151–223.

50 See Barron, "New Hampshire's Secret Modernism," 66–70. For Frost's remarks on footnotes, see Helen Bacon, "Frost and Ancient Muses," 77.

Mourning Old Hampshire in New Hampshire:
Robert Frost's Ongoing Conversation with Edward Thomas

Marissa Grunes
The University of Colorado Boulder

Robert Frost spent August 1914 walking through the Gloucestershire countryside with Edward Thomas, whom he had met the previous fall. Their friendship lasted fewer than three years, yet was deeply significant to both writers. Soon after Frost returned to the US, Thomas enlisted in the Artists Rifles and deployed to France to fight in World War I. He was killed by a shell in Arras, France, on Easter Monday in 1917, a copy of Frost's *Mountain Interval* among his effects.

New Hampshire, which appeared in 1923, was the first collection Frost published after Thomas's death, and it bears the stamp of this loss. Frost had previously told friends that he couldn't write about Thomas, as the grief was "too near"; he found that something in him "refuses to take the risk—angrily refuses to take the risk—of seeming to use a grief for literary purposes."[1] *New Hampshire* departs from that silence. The collection contains two poems clearly associated with Thomas: "Not to Keep" (about a soldier home on leave) and "To E.T.," Frost's only elegy dedicated to a named individual.[2] Around these more overtly elegiac poems, Frost also builds a series of meditations on loss. Several of these poems pay subtle homage to Thomas, including two—"Dust of Snow" and "The Need of Being Versed in Country Things"—that bear close formal and thematic resemblance to poems by Thomas. Taken together, these poems suggest a particular elegiac approach: the ongoing effort of one poet to resurrect and sustain the life of a brother poet, whose presence had been vital to the poet's own meaning-making.

Shortly after Thomas's death, Frost wrote to a mutual friend: "Edward Thomas was the only brother I ever had. I fail to see how we can have been so much to each other, he an Englishman and I an American and our first meeting put off till we were both in middle life. I hadn't a plan for the future that didn't include him."[3] When the two met "in middle life," both were wondering what to make of a diminished thing: lives each found unsatisfying and already half-over, lived amid a modernity rapidly encroaching on their beloved rural places. Frost had recently published his second book of poetry, while Thomas had published over a dozen books of prose, and hundreds of review articles, establishing himself as one of the most prolific and well-respected poetry critics in the UK. Yet despite having confided to his friend Walter de la Mare that he wished to write poetry,[4] he did not take the plunge into verse until the fall of 1914, shortly after he and Frost had become close friends.[5]

Critics have tended to give Frost credit for the substantial body of poetic work Thomas composed between November 1914 and his death in 1917. Yet Frost steadily resisted this view over the decades that followed, insisting that he and Thomas met as equals whose ideas had already begun to develop along parallel tracks; he understood that Thomas's "November" was the early poem of a mature writer. Indeed, influence traveled in both directions, and Thomas—his writing, his friendship, and his death—left a lasting imprint on Frost. In exploring the poetics of friendship between these two men, we would do well to try what few of Frost's contemporaries did, and take seriously his insistence that the two met as equals. This approach leads us to what Edna Longley perceptively calls Frost's "continuing dialogue with Thomas."[6] We might also call this an ongoing conversation, picked up where they left off on their "walks-talking" through the English countryside. Thomas's absence seems to have deprived Frost of an ideal reader: the sort of interlocutor whose attention and response gave significance to Frost's verbal expression. In letters about and elegiac poems for Thomas, Frost used language to bind the pair together "in a relation of elected friends," as he would write in his late poem "Iris by Night." At the same time, in Frost's poems that have Thomas in mind, language gives way to nonverbal forms of connection—as in Thomas's own work, which celebrates visionary experiences appreciated in silence.

While much of Frost's work has an elegiac tone, Guy Rotella notes that "Frost mostly avoided elegy."[7] Frost's resistance to elegizing Thomas—or indeed any of the friends and family he lost throughout his life—reflects what Jahan Ramazani identifies as the "economic problem of mourning," a sense of guilt at "reap[ing] aesthetic profit from loss."[8] Yet, as Rotella demonstrates, Frost sustains the "vestiges"[9] of what Ramazani calls that "ancient literary dialogue with the dead"[10]—and nowhere so intensively, I would contend, as in his ongoing conversation with Thomas. Rotella points to Frost's use of consolatory elegiac tropes laid out by Peter Sacks—the regrowth of vegetative life and natural cycles of rebirth, images of weaving or other forms of creation—in poems across Frost's oeuvre, including "To E.T." and "The Need of Being Versed in Country Things." However, where traditional elegiac imagery may result from what Sacks calls the "substitutive turn or act of troping that any mourner must perform,"[11] I would suggest that the more potent substitute with which Frost seeks to connect in these and other poems is the covert presence of Thomas's own writing. It is through Frost's responses to Thomas's poetry—to which Frost helped give birth—that the surviving poet makes his strongest attempts to preserve the life and mind of his friend. No other person in Frost's life receives such treatment.

Frost's ongoing dialogue with Thomas's work, which runs through *New Hampshire* and beyond, suggests his unwillingness to let Thomas's artistic influence fade. Frost's responses to Thomas represent an attempt to keep the dead alive, but not ultimately to bridge the gap between denial and acceptance of loss as in traditional elegy—instead, Frost means Thomas to remain a constant companion to his thoughts. At the same time, while such visionary poems as "Iris by Night" make clear that Frost does not join with other modern elegists in "scorning recovery and transcendence," he does fiercely refuse to "abandon the dead."[12] Three decades after Thomas's death, Frost still imagines what he might "ponder" with Thomas, and frames questions to ask his dead friend.[13] In seeking poetic contact with Thomas, Frost's approach goes beyond the conventional elegiac desire to immortalize the deceased. More urgently, Frost wished to keep Thomas alive for himself: to revive Thomas as an imaginative companion whose conversation and insights he valued. His poetry honoring Thomas is therefore not only for the ages but for his own lifetime.

Frost and Thomas: Continuing the Dialogue

The notion that Thomas owed his poetic inspiration, voice, and development to Frost emerged soon after Thomas's death. In his review of Thomas's posthumous *Poems*, Louis Untermeyer discusses Thomas's poetry primarily by way of unfavorable comparisons to Frost's work. The essay irked Frost. In a letter to his daughter Lesley in 1920, Frost writes: "Louis means to be a good backer. It's funny to watch him, though, when its a question of Edward Thomas. He parts company with me there. He refuses to like Thomas' poetry and he refuses to like my poetry to Thomas [the elegiac poem "To E.T."]. Funny world."[14] "Funny world" was one of Thomas's favorite catchphrases, which he used in his final letter to Frost; it surfaces in Frost's letters when Thomas is on his mind, as though Frost wishes to ventriloquize his friend or allow him to respond in his own words.[15]

Given the decades Thomas spent writing prose—most of which Untermeyer dismisses as "hack-work"[16]—it is hard to credit the idea that he owes his poetic voice entirely to Frost. Yet the idea persisted. When Mark Van Doren came to review Thomas's *Collected Poems* in *The Nation* in 1921, he began by remarking that "it is pretty well known how Robert Frost, going over to England in 1912, found the overworked critic and hack in the middle of his fourth decade and drew such poetry out of him as he had time to yield before the war took his life in 1917."[17] Frost delicately expresses his frustration in a letter:

> Of course I am pleased to have Edward Thomas' name connected with mine, as I think he would be. One has to be careful to put it just the right way. I didnt show him how to write. All I did was show him himself in what he had already written. I made him see that much of his prose was poetry that only had to declare itself in form to win him a place where he belonged among the poets.[18]

This phrasing closely echoes a letter around the same time to Grace Hazard Conkling, a professor who was developing lectures connecting Frost and Thomas's poetry:

> I am grateful that you should have thought to link Edward Thomas' name with mine in one of your lectures. You will be careful, I know, not to say anything to exalt either of us at the expense of the other. There's a story going round that might lead you to exaggerate our debt to each other. Anything we may be thought to have in common we had before we met. When [Ralph] Hodgson introduced us at a coffee house in London in 1913 I had written two and a half of my three books, he had written all but two or three of his thirty.[19]

Frost emphasizes Thomas's astounding productivity, averring that Thomas was "a poet all in his own right. The accent is absolutely his own." He goes on the declare the radical equality of their friendship. "There was never a moment's thought about who may have been influencing whom," Frosts insists. "The least rivalry of that kind would have taken something from our friendship. We were greater friends than almost any two ever were practicing the same art."[20]

It is a curious question why no one would take the poet at his word. Even today, scholars tend to look for the Frostian strain in Thomas, rather than asking what Frost might have learned from this friend who was, after all, the more prolific writer. The ambiguous composition histories and ironic distance characterizing Frost's poetry admittedly make it difficult for critics swimming against the current to establish direct influence, although Longley has identified prose passages by Thomas that may have provided Frost with material.[21]

Frost's statements about Thomas repeatedly strike two notes: gratitude for being "linked" with Thomas and caution to be "careful" in framing that connection. Perhaps surprisingly for so competitive a writer, Frost's version of the narrative suggests an alternative framing to one of influence or rivalry: that of dialogue. As I noted above, as late as 1948 Frost laments the fact that Thomas is not there to "ponder" ideas with him, and two years later he reportedly insisted to Untermeyer that he and Thomas had been "perfect friends"[22]—perhaps alluding to Thomas's line about the "trees and us" as "imperfect friends."[23] This sense of reciprocity took poetic form in "Iris by Night." While the poem was written after *New Hampshire* appeared, a quick glance will illuminate the dynamic Frost sought with his fallen friend. Frost published this masterpiece of poetic friendship in 1937, evidently in belated answer to Thomas's 1916 poem about their time together, "The sun used to shine." The poem responds to Thomas as though to carry on an interrupted conversation—one not over, but simply paused (as he writes in his elegy "To E.T.") by "some delay."

"Iris by Night" begins with an evening walk when, "one another's guide," Thomas and Frost go "groping down a Malvern side," evidently somewhat hapless but happy in the absence of a single leader. The poem is dominated by sun and moon, as though in response to the centrality of those celestial bodies in Thomas's "The sun used to shine." Thomas's title suggests an earlier golden summer now darkened by war, whose violence Thomas often associates in his writing with nighttime and the moon "which soldiers in the east afar / Beheld then."[24] Frost's answering poem is a moonlit one, as though the survivor is reluctant to place himself under the sun now lost to his friend. The only sun in "Iris by Night" is a visionary "former sun" whose intermingled "fragments" create a mystical spectacle of "confusing lights." Frost seems to imagine himself and his friend as these solar fragments that in some reincarnated future will "concentrate anew and rise as one." Like the lovers in Plato's *Symposium*, these two men are parts of a mystical whole; indeed, writing about Thomas in 1921 Frost had insisted in Platonic fashion that "what we had in common we had from before we were born."[25]

The mystically watery scene that follows may remind us of Thomas's 1914 essay "This England," which he adapted into "The sun used to shine." There, moonrise leaves Thomas "deluged" with the certainty that he can only truly claim to love England if he is prepared to die for it. Frost seems to render this metaphor literally in "Iris by Night," where mystical waters bring on a revelatory vision, turning Frost's own moonlit scene magically "submarine"—a subtle reminder of war and perhaps also recalling the watery deaths in two of the language's most famous elegies, Milton's *Lycidas* and Tennyson's *In Memoriam*. The moment of greatest poetic intensity is marked by silence, though, as are so many of Thomas's most powerful poetic moments.[26] It occurs by tacit grace of a moonbow that lifts itself from the ground and circles the friends beyond "all division time or foe can bring."[27] Like the "confusing lights" that Frost imagines reincarnated into a whole, or like the command in the later wartime poem "Directive," the two here become briefly "whole again beyond confusion."

Frost is often described as a competitive poet, jealous of rivals.[28] With Thomas, he seemed to reach for a different dynamic—one that would avoid the fraught questions of who influenced whom or who was the greater poet. The tendency of Thomas's readers to laud Frost, together with the fact that Thomas was incapable of answering those readers, may have made the line easier for Frost to hold. At the same time, Thomas had achieved the battlefield death Frost could only talk about; if anything, that death may have cemented Thomas in Frost's firmament as the sort of man with whom Frost might be proud to connect himself. Indeed, Frost responded to Thomas's enlistment by imagining his own, writing in 1915: "You are doing it for the self-same reason I shall hope to do it for if my time ever comes and I am brave enough, namely, because there seems nothing else for a man to do."[29] As Cubeta observes, Thomas's "decision to be both a poet and a soldier" marked "what would really endure in that friendship" for Frost.[30] Cubeta points to Frost's lifelong investment in the idea of a "heroic life" in which "fear . . . must be met by vigorous and courageous responses."[31] Thomas's reluctance to join would have made the decision all the more courageous to Frost. Not two months after Thomas enlisted, Frost applauded the choice to a mutual friend, remarking: "I think it [the war] has made some sort of new man and a poet out of Edward Thomas."[32] At the same time, Frost acknowledged his status as a military outsider to Thomas in a letter of November 1916: "Talk is almost too cheap when all your friends are facing bullets. I don't believe I ought to enlist (since I am of course an American), but if I can't enlist, at least I refuse to talk sympathy beyond a certain point."[33] Frost's excuse sounds facile given how many Americans volunteered, but his refusal to "talk sympathy" may reflect the same ethical scruples that held him off from elegy.

Elegy in *New Hampshire*: "To E.T."

The elegy "To E.T." is the keystone of *New Hampshire*'s ongoing conversation with Thomas of Old Hampshire.[34] Frost was no stranger to death even before he met Thomas, having lost his mother and two of his children in the early 1900s. Frost was also called upon to honor other poets during his long life. Why did only Thomas receive an elegy? Thomas's death seems to have touched Frost's poetic life in a singular way. In life, philosophy, and language, the two were "one another's guide," as Frost wrote in "Iris by Night." Thomas's premature death left the survivor with a sense of things—relationships, lives, even a war— dangling in media res. "To E.T." gives play to incompletion as a strategy for keeping Thomas's presence alive in the mind of the surviving poet.

In "To E.T.," Frost emphasizes reciprocity between the two men. This mirroring especially appears around the use of language: as brothers in conversation and as poet-readers of one another's work, each motivated and gave significance to the form taken by the other's verbal creation. In this way, the poem embodies remarks Frost made about the reciprocity between poet and reader; perhaps most famously "no tears in the writer, no tears in the reader,"[35] but also his insistence that an attuned reader cannot stay uninvolved: "The right reader of a good poem can tell the moment it strikes him that he has taken an immortal wound—that he will never get over it."[36]

One thing Frost could not get over was Thomas's style. By contrast with Frost's tendency toward end-stopped lines, "To E.T." takes up Thomas's extended, heavily enjambed sentences that Frost called "a feat."[37] We might look, for instance, at the opening sentence, which grammatically could conclude at the end of the third line: "I slumbered with your poems on my breast / Spread open as I dropped them half-read through / Like dove wings on a figure on a tomb." Yet the sentence continues for another impressive five lines, generating a sense of suspension and disorientation. After the third line, a reader may be caught off-balance by the turn to an unexpected infinitive clause; one wonders when the grammatical units will resolve. The "tomb" at the end of the third line thus becomes a false ending, conjuring the story of disciples rolling back the stone from Christ's burial chamber on Easter Day Like a disciple, Frost keeps the spirit of his friend—killed on Easter Monday—alive beyond the tomb.

Frost does so by positioning himself and his dead friend as mirrored images. When Frost describes himself slumbering "with your poems on my breast...like dove wings on a figure on a tomb," he may have in mind the edition of Thomas's poems released by Frost's own publisher Holt in 1917, which is dedicated "To Robert Frost"—a gesture echoed by the title of Frost's elegy. In the symbolism of tomb effigies, the dove represents the Holy Spirit, a figure of divine inspiration. Here, the book is left lying open, just as Thomas's life was interrupted, an unfinished book. The half-read book is also a half-written one. The small joke hidden in this image—Frost has fallen asleep reading his friend's poems—may also reflect Frost's guilt at not having done enough for his friend in life.[38] While Thomas had lived, Frost had been a poor correspondent; in 1920, shortly after "To E.T." was first published, Frost wrote to Wilbur Cross, editor of the Yale Review, that "anything you can say or do to keep him from being forgotten helps me pay the debt of friendship I owe him."[39]

At the same time, Frost seems to follow the example of Thomas's poems in moving toward visionary communion. Thomas's poems often turn to birdsong or even silence as an alternative form of knowing. In "Sedge-Warblers," a poem with parallels to Frost's "The Oven-Bird,"[40] Thomas describes these birds whose song "lacks all words, all melody" yet who go about "Wisely reiterating endlessly / What no man learnt yet, in or out of school." Frost was attuned to this aspect of his friend's thought. In a letter of 1928, Frost describes a passage from Helen Thomas's memoir *As It Was*, in which Thomas reportedly remarked, "We are knowing, but the nightingale knows all."[41] "To E.T." seems to acknowledge the way Thomas's poems guide readers toward an almost mystical fascination with wordlessness, as Frost hopes that reading Thomas's poems will unite them in a dream-vision. Indeed, in Thomas's descriptions of their friendship, some of the most intimate moments—as between any two lovers—are wordless. In "The sun used to shine," for instance, Thomas writes of "talks / And silences" between the two friends.[42] Frost, however, who would speak decades later of how he and Thomas "tired the sun down with talking on the footpaths and stiles of Leddington and Ryton," cannot seem to let the silence alone.[43] He hopes in his visionary sleep to exchange dream-words with his friend and carry on their conversation.

Frost further mirrors Thomas by turning himself into a recumbent tomb effigy—either for his departed friend or himself—and thereby directing his elegiac energies toward his own death. Taking up an elegiac tradition with roots in Milton's *Lycidas*, reportedly Frost's favorite poem,[44] the surviving poet sees his own mortality prefigured in his fellow-poet's death. Frost goes on to highlight their relation as poet-readers of one another's work. Frost writes: "I meant, you meant, that nothing should remain / Unsaid between us, brother." Yet so many things do remain unsaid. In a letter of October 1920, Frost wrote to his and Thomas's mutual friend John Haines, "Well, the war is over. I don't know that I have said that to you yet. (We'll neither of us ever say it to Edward Thomas.)"[45]

That silence seems to leave the war unfinished. Frost addresses Thomas in the elegy: "when you fell that day / The war seemed over more for you than me, / But now for me than you—the other way." In this paradoxical chiasmus, Thomas's war ended with his death, yet also persists indefinitely because Thomas was not able to experience the war's true resolution on Armistice Day. Frost lived to see the war over in a way Thomas did not. Yet Thomas's absence also deprives Frost of a sense of finality: he wonders how the war could truly be

> . . . over, though, for even me who knew
> The foe thrust back unsafe beyond the Rhine,
> If I was not to speak of it to you
> And see you pleased once more with words of mine?

What is the importance of pleasing Thomas with words? Frost says various words to please Thomas in the poem. He shares the message that the enemy has been pushed out of France and defeated. He also calls Thomas a "soldier, then poet, then both," recognition of two roles into which Frost believed he helped push Thomas.[46] Frost also seems to be thinking of Thomas's pleasure at Frost's poetic words, perhaps even expressing gratitude for Thomas's reviews of *North of Boston*, which boosted Frost's reputation and were some of the first reviews to please Frost.[47] If news of victory and the title "poet-soldier" are words to gratify Thomas, the final line also allows for a reciprocal reversal of their roles, in which Frost might be gratified by Thomas's praise for his poetry. While the elegy represents a rare break from Frost's wordless mourning, Eleanor DesPrez points to this final stanza as revealing Frost's guilty awareness that elegy is ultimately self-serving. It turns "back upon the survivor," as she notes: "the loss he cannot assimilate is the loss of a witness to his own life and work."[48] At the same time, there is a disarming pathos in Frost's desire—even after the blockbuster sales of *North of Boston* and amid a stream of honors and acclaim[49]—to hear praise from this one particular reader. Any elegiac consolation to result from the poem seems embedded in this wish—just out of reach—to share the rewards of language, through the tight coupling of reader and poet.

Poetic Brotherhood in *New Hampshire*

The poems surrounding this elegy in the collection also consider compensatory possibilities. "To E.T." is bookended by "Dust of Snow" and "Nothing Gold Can Stay," which Cubeta notes share themes of "transiency of nature and life" also touched on in Thomas's "The sun used to shine."[50] These poems join several others in carrying Thomas's presence through the collection, including "Not to Keep," "To Earthward," and "The Need of Being Versed in Country Things."

In all of these cases, a direct line of influence is difficult to trace. Two poems in particular—"Dust of Snow" and "The Need of Being Versed in Country Things"—bear close resemblance to poems Thomas sent to Frost, "Thaw" and "Aspens." In both cases Frost provided composition dates preceding those of Thomas's poems, but he is not known to have circulated the poems until after Thomas's death. Thomas never mentions either poem by Frost. Other poems present similar difficulties. "Not to Keep" tells a story of a soldier home on leave for war, which has prompted critics to see Thomas's wife Helen in the role of the wife receiving her soldier.[51] Yet Frost claimed to have written "Not to Keep" in 1914, and his wife Elinor dated it between 1913 and 1915.[52] Indeed, in a letter of December 1914 Frost expands on the suffering of recovering soldiers being sent back to the front.[53] These dates would put its composition before Thomas had even enlisted in the Artists Rifles. Thomas sent Frost his own tonally quite different poem on this subject, "Home," in March 1916,[54] just ten days after Frost gave Wilbur Cross permission to publish "Not to Keep."[55] A few months later Thomas mentions having received "Not to Keep" enclosed in a letter of May 1, possibly in response to "Home"—though Frost's letter has not been found.[56] In other words, the two men could have written the poems in parallel, with no awareness of the other.

Meanwhile, "To Earthward," one of *New Hampshire*'s signature poems and one Frost identified as a turning point for him—and one so painful that he avoided reading it in public[57]—bears similarities to Thomas's "The Owl." In both poems, the speaker discovers a need to "salt" experience with alertness to suffering. Here again, Frost's poem was written earlier, in the summer of 1914.[58] Yet, like these other poems, "To Earthward" is part of *New Hampshire*'s elegiac tapestry. It was apparently composed as Frost's relationship with Thomas flourished, and is marked by qualities—a brooding tone, an emphasis on the physicality of the body and the earth's soil—that may be signs of Thomas's influence.

In all of these cases, neither poet mentions the parallel compositions in any letter scholars have found. The assertions of early composition dates would protect Frost from the accusation of being derivative; the early dates would also have given him the pleasure of muddling critical assessments of his poetic development—which he did by publishing early poems alongside late ones, giving himself an air of timeless mastery.[59] Regardless, Frost's publishing decisions are significant. If the dates are accurate, Frost evidently waited almost a decade to collect these poems. Their inclusion in *New Hampshire* contributes to the collection's elegiac mood and suggests that—even leaving aside the question of influence—they belong to the ongoing conversation Frost sought with Thomas.[60] Frost could not have missed the parallels with his friend's poems, and their placement carries Thomas's memory through the pages.

"Dust of Snow" appears just before "To E.T." and sets up the potential for consolation amid grief or regret. It exhibits noticeable thematic and formal similarities to Thomas's "Thaw," which Frost received in a letter of March 1916 and which subsequently appeared in Thomas's 1917 volume dedicated to Frost. In Frost and Elinor's later attempts to recall composition dates, they place "Dust of Snow" at 1906 and between 1900 and 1910 respectively, yet Andrew Angyal found an unpublished manuscript version titled "A Mercy," which he describes as apparently written after 1915, and Jeffrey Cramer notes that in a letter of November 1920, a month before it appeared as "A Favour" in the *London Mercury*, Frost contrasts this poem with one composed much earlier.[61] "Dust of Snow has no traps for the unwary chronologists," Frost wrote. "It is simply a little poem done rather recently by me about as I am."[62] Perhaps, like its neighbor "Nothing Gold Can Stay," the poem was conceived earlier and completed in 1920.[63] Leaving composition history aside, Thomas's "Thaw" bears an unmistakable resemblance to "Dust of Snow":

> Over the land freckled with snow half-thawed
> The speculating rooks at their nests cawed
> And saw from elm-tops, delicate as flowers of grass,
> What we below could not see, Winter pass.

"Dust of Snow" is composed in almost the same form but broken into loose iambic dimeter lines:

> The way a crow
> Shook down on me
> The dust of snow
> From a hemlock tree
>
> Has given my heart
> A change of mood
> And saved some part
> Of a day I had rued.

Both poems center on a corvid (a rook and crow respectively) perched during winter in a tree historically associated with death (Thomas's elm and Frost's hemlock).[64] In each case the speaker stands below the tree, where the bird of ill omen offers a gift of vision or pleasure that lifts the speaker's despairing mood. The poems are formally akin as well. If one stitches together each pair of lines in Frost's poem, one arrives back at Thomas's AABB rhyme scheme, which had already incorporated some internal rhyme. Indeed, Frost's line breaks appear roughly where Thomas's prepositional phrases or appositives naturally create a pause at each hemistich, creating a neatly matching pace. Frost noted that his poem "is all one sentence,"[65] and while Frost has used a more straightforward grammatical structure than does Thomas, in each poem the single sentence's predicate emerges in the second half, allowing for a small twist at the end.

Thomas's brief, riddling poem is marked by uneasy optimism. The speaker is among the "we" below, caught in the despair of unending winter, yet the poem also grants a rook's eye view of a more hopeful prospect. This elevated vision starts in the first line, with its description of the land "freckled with snow" as though seen from high up. The rooks are perched on elms, "delicate as flowers of grass," as though the poet were imagining an even loftier consolatory view of spring flowers and rejuvenation. The possibility of solace also emerges from temporal telescoping: the rooks can see not only space but also time over a wider, perhaps supernatural, scale. The "speculating" rooks—from *specula*, Latin for "watchtower"—have a literal vantage from the top of their elm, a tree classically associated with warfare and death in Homer and Virgil. The rooks also call to mind the ravens of Norse mythology, Huginn (from Old Norse for "thought") and Muninn (from Old Norse for "memory" or "mind"), who perch on the All-Father Odin's shoulders. The "speculating" rooks may represent the poet's power to look beyond physical and emotional actualities. Like the poet, these rooks both "saw" and "cawed": they watch and speak.

Frost's bird of death, perched on a tree with an ill-starred name, also brings a surprising promise of life—but rather than looking to the future, the poem celebrates the present moment. It vividly captures an instant in time, as the dislodged snow seems to "shake" the speaker himself out of melancholy and into an observant communion with living things around him. The arrangement of a black corvid amid white snow offers the contemplative starkness of a woodcut or haiku, reinforced by the speaker's response: one can imagine him pausing mid-stride, drawn out of distracted musings to a sudden, clear vision. The poem itself reflects that clarity, capturing a complex scene in few brisk strokes. This little verse is like a talisman, a consolatory moment bound up by the ribbon of its dimeter rhymes.

While Thomas Hardy chooses the innocent thrush to sing amid the "Frost . . . spectre-grey" of "Some blessed Hope, whereof he knew / And I was unaware," these two poets turn instead to much-maligned corvids. It is difficult for a reader not to think of Shakespeare's "rooky wood" where Macbeth imagines his hired assassins meeting their victims, as well as Poe's "The Raven," which Frost knew by heart from childhood.[66] The trees too are heavy with symbolism: hemlock shares a name with the flowering shrub that poisoned Socrates, while the elm has a venerable literary tradition stretching back to the *Iliad* where it is planted on the tombs of great warriors. In one Homeric legend, an elm above the grave of the first Greek killed at Troy grew so tall that its top leaves could see the city's far-off walls; these leaves perpetually wilted and died out of bitterness. More humbly, Thomas Gray describes how the "rude forefathers of the hamlet sleep" beneath a "rugged elm" in his "Elegy Written in a Country Churchyard." Frost and Thomas play on traditional tropes of death and violence, blending knowledge of literary antecedents with the possibility of a fresh encounter with these birds and trees as they exist in the natural world, unfettered by literary baggage. Indeed, in the prose volume *In Pursuit of Spring*, which Frost greatly admired,[67] Thomas frequently notes the presence of rooks at the top of elm trees; he hardly mentions rooks without pairing them to their favorite haunt.[68]

These allusions, along with the poems' syntax, allow pain to lurk beneath a solace only partly successful. Thomas's final line leaves a reader unsure whether to trust the lowly human or elevated rook's vision, and Frost's crow can only save "some part" of the day; the speaker's regretful "rue" still closes the poem. When Frost retitles the poem for *New Hampshire*, his "favour" becomes the "dust" of the burial service in the Book of Common Prayer: "ashes to ashes, dust to dust, in sure and certain hope of the Resurrection to eternal life."[69]

Frost's concern for Thomas's own eternal life appears in the elegy that directly follows. The "day I had rued" in "Dust of Snow" is echoed by what in "To E.T." Frost refers to as "that day" when Thomas "fell." In "To E.T.," Frost implies his fear that the winter of loss will never pass for him, just as the war will never truly end for Thomas, killed in the middle of it. If the resulting association with

Thomas helps us conjure "Thaw" as this poem's poetic twin, it may also serve to acknowledge the quiet way in which "Thaw" expresses the profound courage of a frightened man facing up to history and death—as Thomas did in joining the Army. Frost appreciated the cost of that decision, as he lets Thomas know in a letter responding to the news: "You have let me follow your thought in almost every twist and turn toward this conclusion. I know pretty well how far down you have gone and how far off sideways. And I think the better of you for it all. Only the very bravest could come to the sacrifice in this way."[70] The man who hoped the rooks might see what he could not, joined the seemingly endless conflict of World War I against the grain of his temperament. Perhaps Frost found some consolation in Thomas's rook that can see winter pass from high above the bleak, limited lives of men, though his own approach is more modest: a crow that allows some small joy—a dusting of snow, a poem by a friend—to fall to earth.

That motion of falling, which carries through "Dust of Snow" and "To E.T.," culminates with the Edenic fall in the poem that immediately follows the elegy in *New Hampshire*, "Nothing Gold Can Stay." Frost reported that he wrote the first stanza of this poem in 1900 and the second stanza in 1920,[71] meaning that the poem's expansion into the moral dimensions of innocence and mortality emerged during the same year in which he finished and published many poems connected with Thomas. While "Nothing Gold" may not respond directly to Thomas's work, its placement in the collection draws it into dialogue with Thomas's memory. The poem, with its theme of lost innocence, thus rounds out this elegiac trio honoring Thomas and his dawning poetic career.

Believing the Phoebes Wept

Frost closes *New Hampshire* with "The Need of Being Versed in Country Things," an apt manifesto for the poetic ideas born out of his years farming in New Hampshire, but also a poem that tacitly conjures Thomas's memory. In content and form this poem resembles Thomas's "Aspens," which in July 1915 Frost had called the "loveliest of all."[72] Five years later, in an April 1920 letter to Untermeyer that also mentions "To E.T.," Frost notes that Untermeyer has never seen his poem "The Importance of Being Versed in New England Ways," which ends "But one had to be versed in New England Ways / Not to believe the Phoebes wept."[73] Like "Dust of Snow," the poem first appeared in 1920 but may have been conceived much earlier. In 1930, Frost marked this poem as having been composed in 1900[74]—yet he was evidently still fiddling with it in 1920 when he wrote to Untermeyer.

Frost had opened his previous collection *Mountain Interval* with a poem poking mild fun at Thomas's indecision and self-seriousness, "The Road Not Taken." In that poem, the Thomas-like speaker expects to recall his evidently insignificant youthful decisions "with a sigh / Somewhere ages and ages hence." Frost had shown this poem to Thomas in early 1915 but backed away from his teasing after Thomas seemed to worry over and criticize the poem.[75] Their awkward exchange—when accompanied by Thomas's shame at his own frightened reaction to an angry gamekeeper the two encountered in England—may have contributed to Frost's concern that he had inadvertently hardened Thomas's resolve to join the Army.[76] Any bad feelings must have been forgotten when Thomas wrote to Frost in January 1917 that reading *Mountain Interval* had meant "getting close to you again."[77] Frost could not help but be moved by the knowledge that Thomas brought the volume with him to France.[78] "The Need of Being Versed"—whose speaker hears "the sigh we sigh / From too much dwelling on what has been"—acts as a poignantly playful answering poem that closes not only *New Hampshire* but the era of Frost's life in which his friendship with Thomas flourished.

Both Thomas's "Aspens" and "The Need of Being Versed" are composed of six quatrains whose second and fourth lines rhyme. The two poems even share some end rhymes and one almost identical rhyming pair: compare Thomas's "road / abode" with Frost's "road / load" as well as Thomas's "out of the inn / these fifty years have been" with Frost's "out and in / dwelling on what has been." Both poems also address the same theme in an almost identical setting: nonhuman beings (aspens and phoebes, respectively) seem to mourn a lost way of life, represented by an abandoned rural building. In both cases, the poet may know better than to attribute mourning to the nonhuman thing (whether tree or bird), yet is drawn to the pathetic fallacy nonetheless. Here are the two poems side by side:

Aspens

All day and night, save winter, every weather,
Above the inn, the smithy, and the
shop,
The aspens at the cross-roads talk
together
Of rain, until their last leaves fall
from the top.

Out of the blacksmith's cavern
comes the ringing
Of hammer, shoe, and anvil; out of
the inn
The clink, the hum, the roar, the
random singing—
The sounds that for these fifty years
have been.

The whisper of the aspens is not
drowned,
And over lightless pane and footless road,
Empty as sky, with every other
sound
Not ceasing, calls their ghosts from
their abode,

A silent smithy, a silent inn, nor
fails
In the bare moonlight or the thick-
furred gloom,
In tempest or the night of
nightingales,
To turn the cross-roads to a ghostly room.

And it would be the same were no
house near.
Over all sorts of weather, men, and
times,
Aspens must shake their leaves and
men may hear

**The Need of Being Versed in
Country Things**

The house had gone to bring
again
To the midnight sky a sunset
glow.
Now the chimney was all of the
house that stood,
Like a pistil after the petals go.

The barn opposed across the way,
That would have joined the house
in flame
Had it been the will of the wind,
was left
To bear forsaken the place's
name.

No more it opened with all one
end
For teams that came by the stony
road
To drum on the floor with scurrying hoofs
And brush the mow with the
summer load.

The birds that came to it through
the air
At broken windows flew out and
in,
Their murmur more like the sigh
we sigh
From too much dwelling on what
has been.

Yet for them the lilac renewed its
leaf,
And the aged elm, though
touched with fire;
And the dry pump flung up an
awkward arm;
And the fence post carried a
strand of wire.

Whatever wind blows, while they
and I have leaves
We cannot other than an aspen be
That ceaselessly, unreasonably
grieves,
Or so men think who like a different
tree.

For them there was really nothing
sad.
But though they rejoiced in the nest
they kept,
One had to be versed in country
things
Not to believe the phoebes wept.

But need not listen, more than to my rhymes.

"Aspens" opens by imagining a small town at a cross-roads bustling with sound and activity, later left silent and empty beneath the mournful "whisper of the aspens." The trees whispering over "lightless pane and footless road" create a "ghostly room" that bears the traces of former habitation—not unlike the "Ghost House" of Frost's *A Boy's Will.* Thomas is a poet of sound as much as sight, and here sound allows him to invoke human activity without showing the reader any people, creating a liminal environment populated by unseen presences that readily fade into ghosts.

The sounds of former activity—now silenced by fire and neglect— also haunt the barn in Frost's poem, which repeats (with a difference) Thomas's "inn" / "been" rhyme in its fourth stanza. In that stanza, instead of whispering aspens "calling . . . ghosts from their abode," a reader hears the "murmur" of birds whose sound resembles "the sigh we sigh / From too much dwelling on what has been." "Aspens" is a poem that might itself be guilty of such a sigh: Thomas stresses the poet's identification with the aspens (poet and tree each have "leaves" and each "grieves"), though he acknowledges that those who "like a different tree"—lacking poetic sensibility, perhaps—may see this grieving as "ceaseless" and "unreasonable."

The emphasis in Frost's poem is shifted: he insists that those "versed in country things" should know better than to attribute grief to his phoebes—yet gives their supposed sorrow the poem's last word. "For them there was really nothing sad," the speaker remarks, a turn uniting resentment and relief at these birds' apparent freedom from human sorrow. (A reader may recall the conclusion of "Out, Out—": "And they, since they / Were not the one dead, turned to their affairs.") Thomas's own poems are filled with birds, which he tends to treat in a less ironic and more intimate manner than Frost, allowing their song to represent alternative forms of meaning-making.[79] As in "Iris by Night," Frost also reaches here for classical allusions, choosing a bird whose name carries mythic resonance. The Phoebe of Greek mythology was the Titaness grandmother to Apollo and Artemis, whose sun and moon are at the center of both "The sun used to shine" and "Iris by Night."

Fittingly, the final word of "The Need of Being Versed in Country Things" closes the collection on a note of ambivalent elegy. The conditional statement and negation in the closing two lines create syntax that feels unstable: one must repeatedly return to the penultimate line to remind oneself not to believe the phoebes wept. The grammar demands the mental stubbornness that animates Frost's resistance to elegy, in order to keep the final resonant word from overpowering what comes before it. That very sternness carries its own pathos, and the closing lines seem to flicker between the emotional poles of ironic distance and sorrow. In keeping with the paradox Ramazani explores, the refusal of elegy produces elegy—yet marked by restlessness. Frost's own restlessness drove him to continue reviving Thomas, publishing "A Soldier" in 1927, "Iris by Night" in 1936, and recalling his friend's life and work into his elder years.

All the poetic pairings discussed in this article reflect temperamental differences to which Frost was keenly alive. While Frost's poetry often includes gestures that pull away from melancholy, Thomas more often yields to his tendency toward despair. Thomas himself comes close to apologizing for this trait in a letter that refers to his depressive poem "Rain" as "a form of excrement."[80] A few months later, Frost wrote to Thomas with characteristic bluff irony, "You are so good at black talk that I believe your record will stand unbroken for years to come."[81] Thomas may have even reminded Frost of his wife, Elinor, of whom he would write late in life: "She has been the unspoken half of everything I ever wrote. . . . I have had almost too much of her suffering in this world."[82] Thomas, who "ceaselessly, unreasonably grieves," also carried a sadness Frost understood but feared to indulge. That dynamic may have made Thomas and his poetry an indispensable window onto the world for the tough-minded New Englander.

In the letter in which he praises "Aspens," Frost also responds to Thomas's news that he has enlisted to fight in the war. Frost's response shows a striking awareness of his friend's inner struggle. The sort of indecision and self-torment that Frost had gently mocked in "The Road Not Taken" now takes on a heroic character. Of Thomas's decision to join the Army, Frost writes: "I have never seen anything more exquisite than the pain you have made of it. You are a terror and I admire you." He concludes his praise with the cryptic remark, "All belief is one. And this proves you are a believer."[83] Frost recognized his friend as a man both "versed in country things" and who may also have wanted to believe that the phoebes wept. The emotional flicker that closes *New Hampshire* carries on both sides of the conversation between them.

ACKNOWLEDGMENTS

I am grateful to Robert B. Hass, Calista McRae, Jeremy Mitchell, and Virginia Smith for reading earlier versions of this article with careful and generous attention.

Works Cited

Angyal, Andrew. "Robert Frost's Poetry Before 1913: A Checklist." *Proof: Yearbook of American Bibliographical and Textual Studies* 5 (1977): 67–125.

Cook, Reginald Lansing. *Robert Frost, a Living Voice*. Amherst: University of Massachusetts Press, 1974.

Cramer, Jeffrey S. *Robert Frost Among His Poems: A Literary Companion to the Poet's Own Biographical Contexts and Associations*. Jefferson, NC: McFarland, 1996.

Cubeta, Paul. "Robert Frost and Edward Thomas: Two Soldier Poets." *The New England Quarterly* 52, no. 2 (1979): 147–76.

DesPrez, Eleanor. "'Grief without Grievance': Robert Frost's Modern Elegy." *The Robert Frost Review* 11, no. 11 (2001): 30–50.

Evans, William R. "Robert Frost: The Unpublished Cardinal Letter." *American Literature* 59, no. 1 (1987): 116–18.

Francis, Lesley Lee. *You Come Too: My Journey with Robert Frost*. Charlottesville: University of Virginia Press, 2015.

Frost, Robert. *Collected Poems, Prose & Plays*. Edited by Richard Poirier and Mark Richardson. New York: Library of America, 1995.

————. *The Collected Prose of Robert Frost*. Edited by Mark Richardson. Cambridge, MA: Belknap Press of Harvard University Press, 2007.

————. *The Letters of Robert Frost, Volume 1: 1886–1920*. Edited by Donald Sheehy, Mark Richardson, and Robert Faggen. Cambridge, MA: Harvard University Press, 2014.

————. *The Letters of Robert Frost, Volume 2: 1920–1928*. Edited by Donald Sheehy, Mark Richardson, Robert Bernard Hass, and Henry Atmore. Cambridge, MA: Harvard University Press, 2016.

————. *Selected Letters*. Edited by Lawrance Thompson. New York: Holt, Rinehart and Winston, 1964.

Kendall, Judy. *Edward Thomas: The Origins of His Poetry*. Cardiff: University of Wales Press, 2012.

Hammond, Gerald. "Edward Thomas, Robert Frost and the Uses of Negation." *Proceedings of the British Academy* 90 (1996): 95–127.

Hart, Henry. *The Life of Robert Frost: A Critical Biography*. Chicester, West Sussex: John Wiley & Sons, Inc., 2017.

Hollis, Matthew. *Now All Roads Lead to France: The Last Years of Edward Thomas*. London: Faber and Faber, 2011.

Hornaday, Cullen Pratt. "Outside Modernism: The Friendship and Poetry of Robert Frost and Edward Thomas." *PN Review* 10, no. 1 (1983): 42–46.

Hynes, Samuel. *On War and Writing*. Chicago: University of Chicago Press, 2018.

Leighton, Angela. *Hearing Things: The Work of Sound in Literature*. Cambridge, MA: Harvard University Press, 2018.

Longley, Edna. "An Atlantic Chasm? Edward Thomas and the English Lyric." *Literary Imagination* 16, no. 2 (2014): 233–47.

————. *Poetry in the Wars*. Newcastle upon Tyne: Bloodaxe, 1986.

Parini, Jay. *Robert Frost: A Life*. New York: Henry Holt, 1999.

Pite, Ralph. "Edward Thomas and Robert Frost: To Earthward." In *Anticipatory Materialisms in Literature and Philosophy, 1790–1930*, edited by Jo Carruthers, Nour Dakkak, and Rebecca Spence, 219–40. London: Palgrave Macmillan, 2019.

Ramazani, Jahan. *Poetry of Mourning: The Modern Elegy from Hardy to Heaney*. Chicago: University of Chicago Press, 1994.

Richardson, Mark, ed. *Robert Frost in Context*. Cambridge: Cambridge University Press, 2014.

Rotella, Guy. "Robert Frost and the Vestiges of Elegy." *Literary Imagination* 14, no. 1 (2012): 88–102.

Sacks, Peter. *The English Elegy: Studies in the Genre from Spenser to Yeats*. Baltimore, MD: Johns Hopkins University Press, 1985.

Spencer, Matthew, ed. *Elected Friends: Robert Frost and Edward Thomas: To One Another*. New York: Other Press, 2004.

Stenning, Anna. "'What to Make of a Diminished Thing': Nature and Home in the Poetry of Edward Thomas and Robert Frost 1912–1917." PhD dissertation, University of Worcester, 2014.

Thomas, Edward. *The Annotated Collected Poems*. Edited by Edna Longley. Newcastle upon Tyne: Bloodaxe, 2008.

————. *In Pursuit of Spring*. London: T. Nelson, 1914.

————. *Poems*. New York: Henry Holt and Company, 1917.

Thompson, Lawrance. *Robert Frost, a Biography*. New York: Holt, Rinehart and Winston, 1982.

Untermeyer, Louis. "Edward Thomas." *The North American Review* 209, no. 759 (February 1919): 263–66.

Van Doren, Mark. "Edward Thomas." *The Nation* 113, no. 2944 (1921): 668–69.

Walsh, John Evangelist. *Into My Own: The English Years of Robert Frost, 1912–1915*. New York: Grove Press, 1988.

Wiśniewski, Jacek. *Edward Thomas: A Mirror of England*. Newcastle: Cambridge Scholars, 2009.

ENDNOTES

1   Frost, *Letters, Vol. 1*, 592.
2   Tim Kendall notes the absence of overt elegies beyond "To E.T." (Richardson, *Robert Frost in Context*, 196).
3   Frost, *Letters, Vol. 1*, 552.
4   Leighton, *Hearing Things*, 120.
5   Kendall, *Edward Thomas*, 19.
6   Longley, "An Atlantic Chasm?," 233.
7   Rotella, "Vestiges of Elegy," 88.
8   Ramazani, *Poetry of Mourning*, 6.
9   Rotella, "Vestiges of Elegy," 89.
10 Ramazani, *Poetry of Mourning*, 1.
11 Sacks, *English Elegy*, 5.
12 Ramazani, *Poetry of Mourning*, 4.
13 Frost, *Collected Prose*, 158.
14 Frost, *Letters, Vol. 2*, 32.
15 For Thomas's use of this phrase, see, for instance, Spencer, *Elected Friends*, 188; for Frost's repetitions shortly after Thomas's death, see Frost, *Letters, Vol. 1*, 549, 610, 630. But see also his use in a letter of July 1913 before he met Thomas (*Letters, Vol. 1*, 129). In 1923, he wrote to Wilbur Cross: "It's a funny world, as Edward Thomas and I got so we would say almost simultaneously" (*Letters, Vol. 2*, 326).
16 Untermeyer, "Edward Thomas," 63.
17 Van Doren, "Edward Thomas," 668.
18 Frost, *Letters, Vol. 2*, 212.
19 Frost, *Letters, Vol. 2*, 172.
20 Frost, *Letters, Vol. 2*, 172–3. Frost on other occasions would go further and assert that Thomas's experience in the Army, more than their friendship, finally formed Thomas into the confident, original poet he became (Frost, *Letters, Vol. 1*, 358). Despite his efforts, Frost found himself up against the same story of his influence on Thomas four years later (see Evans, "Unpublished Cardinal Letter").
21 John Evangelist Walsh is only one scholar of many who since Frost's death have maintained the narrative of "the dramatic development, under Frost's direct influence, of Edward Thomas as a poet" (*Into My Own*, 180), though not all scholars are so blunt. Paul Cubeta in 1979 offered an early assessment of Thomas's impact on Frost, emphasizing Frost's desire to match his "soldier-poet" friend in courage through the rest of his life. Critics such as Cullen Hornaday and Gerald Hammond subsequently treated the two poets as a finely differentiated binary pair who share a complex relationship to their modernist context, while Samuel Hynes goes further in identifying Hardy as the source of their similarities (see Wiśniewski, *Mirror*, 39). More recently, Longley in 2014 urged critics to consider Thomas's influence on Frost and the "consequences . . . for Frost's own poetry." Longley argues that "their literary connection did not end when Thomas was killed," and names "Our Singing Strength" and "Directive" as poems in which "Frost's continuing dialogue with Thomas surfaces" ("Atlantic Chasm," 233), pointing elsewhere to passages in Thomas's prose and poetry that might have inspired these poems (*Annotated Collected Poems*, 148; *Poetry in the Wars*, 45–46). This more balanced approach can be seen in recent studies by Anna Stenning and Ralph Pite, the latter of whom draws fruitful parallels between Thomas's "Digging" and Frost's "To Earthward."
22 Quoted in Hornaday, "Outside Modernism," 42.

23   From Thomas's poem "The Chalk-Pit." All quotes from Thomas's poetry are taken from *The Annotated Collected Poems*; quotes from Frost's poetry are from *The Collected Poems*.

24   See also his essay "This England" (reprinted in Spencer, *Elected Friends*, 31–35) and his poem "The Owl."

25   Frost, *Letters, Vol. 2*, 173.

26   See for instance the moments of potent silence in "The sun used to shine," "Aspens," "Lights Out," "March," and "Home (Often I had . . .)."

27   See Cubeta on the mythic sources for this poem, possibly inspired by Thomas's comment on a rainbow he saw with Frost which was so "pure" it seemed fitting "for a mythologist clad in skins" ("Soldier Poets," 159–160).

28   Lawrance Thompson may have helped establish that reputation (see for example *A Biography*, 26, 297, 335), but other biographers and critics have tended to agree; see for instance Cook, *Living Voice*, 4; Parini, *A Life*, 165; Hart, *Life of Robert Frost*, 58.

29   Frost, *Letters, Vol. 1*, 334.

30   Cubeta, "Soldier Poets," 167.

31   Cubeta, "Soldier Poets," 168–69.

32   Frost, *Letters, Vol. 1*, 358.

33   Frost, *Letters, Vol. 1*, 503.

34   Thomas makes this pun early in their relationship, in a letter of May 1914 (Spencer, *Elected Friends*, 9).

35   Frost, *Collected Prose*, 132.

36   Frost, *Collected Prose*, 88. Frost uses this general remark to launch his roundabout eulogy for Amy Lowell in 1925; it offers insight less into his views on Amy Lowell's work than into the way poetry bridged life and death for Frost, displacing both writer and reader onto the plane of immortality.

37   Frost, *Letters, Vol. 1*, 280.

38   Frost may also have in mind the disciples' failure to stay awake while Christ prayed in the Garden of Gethsemane. I am indebted to Calista McRae for pointing to this parallel, which again places Frost in the position of student to Thomas, rather than teacher.

39   Frost, *Letters, Vol. 2*, 70–71. On several occasions Thomas sounds a note of mild rebuke and hurt at Frost's neglect. In the March 1916 letter that contains "Thaw," discussed here, Thomas remarks: "I had begun to fear perhaps my letters didn't reach you" (Spencer, *Elected Friends*, 126). Frost regretted these lapses, evidently admitting that he "turned out a bad letter writer after I came home. That's the worst. I should have written him twice as many letters as I did write" (quoted in Cubeta, "Soldier Poets," 166).

40   Thomas published "Sedge-Warblers" in *Six Poems* (1916), the same year "The Oven-Bird" appeared in *Mountain Interval*, but he may have started developing the ideas a year earlier (see *Annotated Collected Poems*, 90–91, 240).

41   Frost, *Letters, Vol. 2*, 674.

42   See also the men sitting and looking together in "This England" (Spencer, *Elected Friends*, 33).

43   Frost, *Collected Prose*, 158. If, as Cubeta remarks, "the strategy of "To E.T." is a dream vision that fails," ("Soldier Poets," 170) then the later "Iris by Night" may present a successful vision in which Frost is finally able to let *logos* fall silent in mystical communion.

44   Frost refers to Emerson's "Uriel" as "the best Western poem yet" (*Collected Prose*, 205), but Cook identifies *Lycidas* as Frost's "favorite poem" (*Living Voice*, 107).

45 Frost, *Letters, Vol. 2*, 95.

46 Cubeta points out that Frost reverses chronology by describing Thomas as first a soldier, then a poet, when in fact Thomas became a poet first. "Soldier-poet" better captures a sense of masculine heroism that attracted Frost ("Soldier Poets," 170).

47 See, for instance, Richardson, *Robert Frost in Context*, 276, and Parini, *A Life*, 151.

48 DesPrez, "Grief without Grievance," 37.

49 Parini, *A Life*, 171.

50 Cubeta, "Soldier Poets," 170.

51 Richardson, *Robert Frost in Context*, 195.

52 Angyal, "A Checklist," 101, 104.

53 Frost, *Letters, Vol. 1*, 237.

54 Spencer, *Elected Friends*, 126.

55 Frost, *Letters, Vol. 1*, 430.

56 Spencer, *Elected Friends*, 129.

57 Parini, *A Life*, 224.

58 See Cramer, *Among His Poems*, 80. Thomas wrote his poem in February 1915 (*Annotated Collected Poems*, 198).

59 See Frost's remarks on "Misgiving," apparently written in 1901 (Angyal, "A Checklist," 101) and sent to a friend in its final form in 1913, but not published until 1921 (Frost, *Letters, Vol. 2*, 108, 131, 152).

60 As a rough indicator, the words "death" and "dead" show up twenty-four times in *New Hampshire*, more than in any previous collection and almost twice their frequency in the two previous collections combined. Additionally, we might note other poems in *New Hampshire* without clear links to Thomas but which dwell on wartime and loss: poems such as "The Census-Taker," the chillingly understated "Fire and Ice," the celebrated 1922 lyric "Stopping by Woods on a Snowy Evening," and perhaps most eerily, "Goodbye and Keep Cold," whose garden sinking like a corpse beneath the frozen sod must be "left to God" as it awaits its springtime resurrection.

61 Angyal, "A Checklist," 101, 84; Cramer, *Among His Poems*, 74–75.

62 Frost, *Letters, Vol. 2*, 108.

63 It is also a poem he continued to think about for decades. In 1940 he remarked to a group of friends: "I often feel a special favor to find a flower I have not seen for a long while, or hear a strange bird I haven't heard in years" (quoted in Cramer, *Among His Poems*, 75); over two decades later in 1963 he jotted down an adapted version from memory for a nurse who cared for him (Cramer, *Among His Poems*, 268).

64 I am grateful to Bob Hass for pointing out that *Tsuga canadensis*, the Eastern hemlock, and *Conium maculatum*, or poison hemlock—the flowering shrub that killed Socrates—share little but the Kingdom *Plantae*. The similarity of their common names could not have escaped Frost's notice, though.

65 Quoted in Cramer, *Among His Poems*, 75.

66 Frost's mother loved Poe and her children learned many of his poems by heart when they were young (Thompson, *A Biography*, 48).

67 Frost calls it the "lovliest [sic] book on spring in England" in a letter of 1914 (*Letters, Vol. 1*, 194).

68 Thomas, *In Pursuit of Spring*, 82, 139, 150, 166, 212.

69 While neither Frost nor Thomas engaged personally with organized religion, Frost played on Biblical language (as in "A Servant to Servants"). If he was thinking

about his British friend, he may have found the Book of Common Prayer an apt source.

70   Frost, *Letters, Vol. 1*, 334.

71   Angyal, "A Checklist," 84.

72   Frost may have been alluding to the often-anthologized lyric "Loveliest of Trees" from A.E. Housman's *A Shropshire Lad*. It would be in keeping with Frost's sense of competition to regard his friend's aspens as lovelier still than Housman's "Loveliest of trees, the cherry." Thomas had given Frost's daughter Lesley a copy of the Housman book before the Frosts left England (Francis, *You Come Too*, 64).

73   Frost, *Letters, Vol. 2*, 53.

74   Angyal, "A Checklist," 102.

75   For key parts of this exchange, see Spencer, *Elected Friends*, 49, 61–64, 70. See also Hollis, *Now All Roads Lead to France*, 289.

76   Thomas referred to the gamekeeper repeatedly in his letters before and after he joined the Army, leading Frost to blame (or credit) that incident with prompting Thomas's enlistment (Hart, *Life of Robert Frost*, 176–77; Parini, *A Life*, 155).

77   Spencer, *Elected Friends*, 173.

78   Hollis, *Now All Roads Lead to France*, 312, 336.

79   We might compare the bird in Thomas's "Fifty Faggots" with that in Frost's own woodpile poem "The Wood-Pile." Thomas expresses curiosity about avian internal life, wondering "whatever is forever to a bird"; by contrast, Frost pokes ironic fun at what seems to be the bird's silly, illogical fear. We might also compare the significance of wordless songs, which in Thomas's "Sedge-Warblers" are a source of mystical wisdom rather than the ironic deflation of "The Oven-Bird." These differences align with Samuel Hynes's point that Thomas is primarily a "nature" poet while Frost is a "country poet" (*War and Writing*, 344). Thomas's sensitivities lead him to identify more closely with nonhuman creatures, while Frost's emphases lean toward the human. For meaning-making through birdsong, see for instance Thomas's "March," "March the Third," and "Home (Often I had . . .)." Thomas's beloved John Clare may be the only other British poet of this era to rival Thomas's obsession with birdsong.

80   Spencer, *Elected Friends*, 126.

81   Frost, *Letters, Vol. 1*, 494.

82   Frost, *Selected Letters*, 450.

83   Frost, *Letters, Vol. 1*, 335.

THE MERCURIAL, ENDURING FRIENDSHIP OF ROBERT FROST AND JAMES HEARST

James F. Hurley
Independent Scholar

"Frost once said, 'you and I are the only two people who are farmers, teachers and poets.'"

In a 1972 magazine interview, the Iowa poet James Hearst (1900–1983) followed his recollection of Robert Frost's ternate description of the two poets with: "Nice compliment but he could be stubborn, so could I."[1] Quite apart from Frost's amusing reassertion of his long-held desire for the credentials of an agrarian—he eventually described himself as "a failed farmer"—the statement reveals Frost's graciousness toward his fellow poet Hearst, only then emerging into regional recognition, and opens the door to an examination of their mutual character traits and their long association. (On top of that, both were baseball pitchers in their youth.)

The author enjoys a humorous remark by Robert Frost at the Iowa Writers Workshop on April 13, 1959. (Photo courtesy of J. Hurley.)

Both were unquestionably teachers, though Hearst taught principally at his hometown college, while Frost was consistently in great national demand for his lectures and readings, often at the nation's marquee universities. Though twenty-six years Frost's junior, Hearst nevertheless was the more seasoned and experienced farmer; his hands and machines had driven more consistently and necessarily into the earth than Frost's. Unlike the dabbling Frost, Hearst was literally born into farming. He and his family made their living for decades on all, or portions of, the five hundred acres first settled by his grandfather in 1859.

Viewed through the vitality and incisiveness of Hearst's most recognized poems, such as "Truth," "Landscape—Iowa," and "The Old Dog," a reader could easily conclude that Hearst's farming career—aided by his brother, Chuck—was continuous, economically rewarding, and skillful, while Frost's was sporadic, often unprofitable, and—without the help of his son, Carol—largely inept.

Like Frost, Hearst's life was marred by tragedy, failure, and loss, including the death of their wives from cancer: Frost's Elinor White in 1938 and Hearst's Carmelita Calderwood in 1951. Unlike Frost, Hearst would again marry happily, to Meryl Norton. But no injury to him was more permanent and seemingly prohibitive than what occurred on Memorial Day, 1919, when he was nineteen years old.

Undated photograph of James Hearst (Courtesy of University of Northern Iowa Special Collections & University Archives.)

Following his discharge from the US Army with the end of World War I, Hearst returned to Iowa State Teachers College (now the University of Northern Iowa) in Cedar Falls. On that fateful national holiday on the eve of the Roaring Twenties, he joined his fraternity buddies for a swim at their favorite spot on the Cedar River to celebrate the semester's final day of classes. Hearst felt "light of foot and fancy free."[2] In past summers, the water's depth at their offshore dock had been a reliable ten feet. Unknown to the youths, the currents of the prior winter had shifted the riverbed to a mere two and a half feet in depth. Hearst, muscular and athletic, was the first to dive. "My head struck the bottom of the river like an explosion," he wrote later. "I opened my eyes in the murky water and drifted with the current, unable to move. 'This is the last of me,' I said to myself."[3] He had broken his back, severely damaging the spinal cord, and would never again walk normally. It was "where footsteps end," he would say.[4]

If there was any mercy to it at all, it would be that a paralytic farmer would plow deeply into verse and become a known and loved regionalist who published some six hundred poems in journals as varied as *Poetry*, *Good Housekeeping*, and the *Iowa State Liquor Store*. He also published ten volumes of poetry and other writings, including an autobiography, a novel, and numerous shorter works. By dint of prodigious and inventive physical effort, he would regain enough strength and mobility in his torso to operate, with Chuck's help, farm machinery with excellent effect—by day asserting his broken body on the crop rows, and by night his revivified imagination on lines of verse. Both would yield a bumper second harvest and, among other literary relationships, a long friendship with Robert Frost.

I nearly left our selfsame hometown of Cedar Falls in the late 1950s without knowing that Hearst, by then earning a reputation as one of the country's ascending regional poets, lived a mere two and a half miles from our family home. I was a liberal arts student and novice poet and writer at Loras College in Dubuque, ninety miles to the east. My first published poem had just appeared in *The Spokesman*, the Loras literary quarterly, and would be given the college's Gerard Manley Hopkins award.

Home from Loras in the summer of 1957 after my junior year, I met Hearst through one of those mysterious life intersections that seem mere happenstance but have lifelong effect when melded with others of its nature. I was introduced to the kind and gentle Hearst through our family friend Edward T. Kelly, a pillar of the community and my employer during high school and college summers. Regrettably, I'd never heard of Hearst, but I have never forgotten him or Ed for their fostering kindness and role modeling.

Ed and I arrived at Hearst's home on a brilliant June afternoon. We parked and walked to his front door, already opened for us. "Come on in," Hearst called out amiably from the living room. He excused himself "for not getting up." Fifty-eight years old, he was big, even sitting in a brown upholstered easy chair. He wore a wool sweater of mixed colors over heavy khaki trousers. His face, deeply cleaved at the cheeks and baked in the kiln of a thousand suns, had the texture of an autumn cornhusk. The knitted sleeves of the sweater ended in hands creased and gnarled, the paralytic fingers turned under for good like the tines of a harrow. We sat down across from him and were offered sweet lemonade by Hearst's wife, Meryl.

"My friend Ed here tells me you like writing," Hearst said.

"Have you had a start?"

Ed answered for me, telling Hearst of my winning poem. "Okay, a good start, then," Hearst said. "Which poets do you like?" I stammered a bit. I wanted to flatter Hearst but had never read his poems and knew little about him. I'd studied Frost, Sandburg, Keats, Wordsworth, Shelley, and others, and heard Ginsberg read from *Howl* in an auditorium in Chicago, but I didn't feel at all competent to answer Hearst with confidence. I quoted a bit of Frost from "Stopping by Woods," never imagining that only two springs later I would sit and talk with Frost at Paul Engle's Iowa Writers Workshop at the University of Iowa.[5]

Ed asked Hearst to read "Truth," Hearst's splendid, seventeen-line metaphor for work and fulfillment. We are invited into the poem to join two neighbor farmers, the speaker, who has plowed his land and—in a corner—heaped a pile of glacial boulders uprisen by winter's bitter Iowa cold, and his adjacent farmer friend, who has yet to plow and asks the question that is answered as the poem begins.

Robert Frost and Paul Engle at the Iowa Writer's Workshop 1959.

Hearst's voice was rhythmic and certain as a whip-poor-will, lowering an octave as he neared the poem's end:

> How the devil do I know
> if there are rocks in your field
> plow it and find out.
> If the plow strikes something
> harder than earth, the point
> shatters at a sudden blow,
> . . . probably
> you hit a rock. That means
> the glacier emptied his pocket
> in your field as well as mine
> but the connection with a thing
> is the only truth that I know of,
> so plow it.

Somehow, being taught the poem by the poet on the poet's land fired and annealed my ear for poetry in a way that would align tone, timbre, and ingenuity when I heard Frost two years later.

We drank another glass of Meryl's lemonade, heard two more poems, chatted again, then rose at Ed's signal to thank our hosts and say goodbye. "Staying at it is the thing about anything," Hearst said as we left. Sitting there across from that teacher and farmer who knew so much of hardness yet stored away silos of bright truth, I began to glimpse what "staying at it" could mean.

Given their personality traits and pursuits-in-common, it is not altogether surprising that a kindred spirit developed between the two poets, most likely sparked by Hearst. In 1933, Frost reportedly received a copy of the manuscript for *Country Men*; it is not certain how Frost came to have the manuscript, but a recently discovered July 8, 1932, letter from Hearst to Frost in South Shaftsbury provides evidence that at least a portion of it came from Hearst himself:

> My interest in your poetry and my high regard for your critical faculty are the reasons for the enclosed verse. There is no one whose judgement I would value more highly, and I trust that I am not imposing when I ask you to comment on my work. Please do not trouble to return them. My hope is that you will be able to find time to go through them at your leisure. With appreciation for any help you will give me, I am,

> Sincerely yours,
> James Hearst.

Earlier in his career, Frost often mentored or otherwise encouraged aspiring poets, but at this point his time was in such great demand that he was unable to respond to all who sought his attention. But he evidently saw enough merit in Hearst's work to respond to *him*. Several months later, after being assured by his and Hearst's mutual friend, Cedar Falls writer and poet Ferner Nuhn, that Hearst was not fishing for a dustjacket endorsement or other public approbation, Frost writes in a letter to Hearst: "You must forgive me if I seem to have taken you too literally when you told me to take my time over your poems. . . . The truth is I read the poems straight through when they came and I have read them all several times. They are true and good poems. Every one is a subject and your note rings clear. I like them very much. Let's be friends on the strength of them and let's see more of each other's work." Frost ended by noting that he had enclosed "one of mine, 'A Bird Singing in Its Sleep'" with the letter.[6]

Hearst carried the letter in his pocket for weeks. Strikingly, though—and likely driven by his pride and stubborn Midwestern independence—he didn't respond to Frost's overture of friendship and offer to trade poems. It appears that the next contact between the two men was not until they met in person early in 1940 in Stone City, Iowa, following a Frost lecture at the nearby University of Iowa. The meeting was arranged by their mutual friend, the poet Paul Engle. The Iowa evening was chilly and Frost relaxed on a hearthside sofa in the spacious home of his host, Dr. George Stoddard. When Hearst entered the room leaning on his brother's arm, Frost turned from his conversation to see who had arrived. Based on his reaction, it was obvious that Frost had been unaware of Hearst's handicap. One of the other guests, Ferner Nuhn, reported that "a look of surprise, and perhaps pity" came to Frost's face.[7] Given Hearst's keen powers of observation and his awareness and anticipation that Frost would be present at the gathering, it is highly probable that—if Frost's expression was indeed piteous—Hearst would have felt it acutely. However—not to quibble—it is likely Frost's considered reaction would have been empathy. As Robert Bernard Hass points out, Frost's narrative poem "The Self-Seeker" ("North of Boston," 1914) was a tribute to Carl Burell, his friend since boyhood, who in 1895 suffered permanent injuries to his legs in a mill saw accident and "would never walk well again and thus never finish the book he had begun on the orchids of New Hampshire."

Unbeknownst to Hearst at the time, Frost wrote to William M. Sloane III, an acquisition editor at Henry Holt & Co., in March 1942 with a recommendation of Hearst's manuscript that was more subdued compared to Frost's outright praise in his much earlier, personal letter to Hearst.[8] "I like them (the poems) rather well though not nearly as well as I like the fellow who did write them," Frost remarked. Frost then described Hearst's infirmity, saying, "I tell you this for obvious reasons, . . . ," then suggests to Sloane that "Henry Wallace mightn't be induced to go on the jacket of his [Hearst's] book with the aim of bringing Hurst [*sic*] out of his regional existence into a national."[9] Early on, Hearst himself was hesitant to reveal to editors that he was handicapped, worrying that they might "publish [him] out of pity." He later remarked, "How little I knew editors!"[10]

It's a good thing that Frost did not write his recommendation to Sloane more promptly, and that Hearst did not become aware of it for two decades, for it certainly would have stung him. Had he read it, the letter likely would have merely hardened his go-it-alone determination. In Hearst's autobiography, in which he expressed his intention to occupy a unique place in American poetry, Hearst must have had Frost at least partially in mind. The Iowan thought "that America had never had a genuine farmer poet . . . to tell the truth about farming and about life as it is lived on a farm . . . corn growing one hundred and twenty-five bushels to the acre."[11]

The most lengthy and personal visit by the two, in late 1940 at Hearst's farm, may be where the rivalry picked up steam, and seems to reveal more than anything about the competitive nuances of their relationship. Frost came to Cedar Falls to lecture at Iowa State Teachers College at the invitation of H. W. Reninger, head of the English department and a friend of Hearst's who hired the poet-farmer to teach there, thus launching Hearst's thirty-four-year career as an educator. At the time, Hearst was forty years old, Frost sixty-six.

"He wanted to see an Iowa farm," Hearst said in his autobiography *My Shadow Below Me*. Reninger suggested a visit to Maplehearst Farm, Hearst's big nearby spread. Hearst and his mother, Katherine, hosted Frost's stay. Hearst recalled, "I had almost enough poems for a book when Robert Frost came to town." This would be Hearst's second book, *The Sun at Noon*; his first, *Country Men*, appeared in 1937 and was critically, if not widely, welcomed.

"Frost, stocky, brown haired and energetic, roamed from barn to fields. He spied a small group of untrimmed, unsprayed apple trees. His face lit up and his voice filled with satisfaction as he said, 'At least we can beat you with apples.'" Hearst had firm opinions about Frost's public identification as a farmer: "I began to think scornfully of Robert Frost as a farmer with a rocky slope farm, a flock of chickens, and one cow. When I met Frost for the first time at our farm, he was equally scornful. 'Too much land in this farm,' he said. 'Mile long corn rows . . .' They roused his indignation."[12] In contrast, Frost's remarks on the productivity of the Iowa soil were generous. "There isn't any way to spoil Iowa corn," he told Hearst. "It's good on the table and in the field. This is good soil. I think I could eat it without having to put it through vegetables first."[13]

Frost's specifications for his morning coffee at the Hearst farm were as precise as his poems. "For breakfast," he told Hearst, I'll have 3 glasses full of 1/3rd coffee, 1/3rd hot water, and 1/3rd hot milk." Of a farm-fresh soft-boiled egg proffered at the breakfast table, Frost commented with characteristic candor, "You should have left the egg in its skin. Maybe I won't use it."[14]

"He wanted dinner at noon," Hearst recalled. "He helped carry out the dishes and complimented Mother on doing her own work. He said,

'That's the way to get it done right.'" "Someone had told him about my poems. Before he went back to town he said to me, 'Get enough poems for a book and send the manuscript to me. I'll pass it on to my publisher.'"

Hearst's reaction was immediate. "I felt patronized, and my own New England blood pulsed in protest. I said, 'Thank you, Mr. Frost, but if I'm going to make it, I'll have to make it on my own.'" According to Hearst, his guest was "stunned" at the seeming ingratitude of his host. "Frost's eyes blazed, his eyebrows bristled, and his lip curled. He turned away abruptly."[15]

Hearst softened in retrospect. "It was a kindly meant and generous offer from one of America's leading poets. It was a helping hand, extended to a young farmer with more aspiration than achievement. But somehow it struck me the wrong way." As Frost departed Maplehearst Farm, he softened as well, according to Hearst, saying to his mother, "Maybe Jim is right. Maybe it is best to make it on your own." "Frost's words," Hearst would write, "stirred me to think about publishing a [another] book of poems."[16] With *The Sun at Noon*, published by Prairie Press located in the decidedly Midwestern town of Muscatine, Iowa, he did just that.

Hearst's poem "The Visit," published in 1962 and dedicated to Frost, brims with relevance when:

> A brown thrush comes to call.
> The short day runs on frozen feet,
> Its shadows lengthen out ahead,
> But today a gentleman in brown
> Sings in our hedge, pecks at our bread. . . .
> The morning climbs it shrunken arch,
> The sundial wakes, but the bird is gone
> As if he had told us all he dared
> Of life renewed by grace of song.[17]

If time does heal all wounds, it may take longer with poets. By at least 1956, however, their mutual regard had warmed and was fixed in place. Although a few critics friendly to Hearst had been calling him the "Robert Frost of the Midwest," Hearst predictably disowned the moniker, and Frost was to visit the Hearst's farm again. Recording the visit, Hearst wrote to Frost: "[My] students the other night said let's skip Yeats and Kipling and spend the whole two hours on the poems of

Frost. I thought you might like to know how we like you here in Iowa. Best wishes and love to you from Mrs. Hearst and myself."[18]

Hearst offered more unsparing praise in an April 1960 letter to Kathleen Morrison: "I wish I could express the deep affection we have for Robert Frost here in Iowa. The whole state welcomes him when he comes to visit us."[19]

Paul Engle, who introduced me to Frost on April 13, 1959, at the University of Iowa's Writers Workshop, was a loyalist to both Frost and Hearst. In praise separated by thirty-three years, he unselfconsciously knits the two together by virtue of their affinities. To commemorate Frost's Iowa visit, Engle's 1941 poem "Robert Frost" was reprinted in the program and excerpted below:

> You give this man the sort of praise
> You give to ripened autumn days
> When the air glows with radiant light
> And leaf fires darken the dense night . . .
> Independent animal,
> Stubborn individual. . .
> On this wind-rounded world the bare
> Loved face hangs like a bruise in air.
> We lift our hands to touch it there.
> If that touch brings pain with delight,
> Joy so great as to give fright,
> it is our life, and it is right.[20]

Similarly, in 1974 Engle wrote the poem "James Hearst" (excerpted below) for a special edition of the *North American Review*:

> . . . a tough and gentle man,
> tongue like a tomahawk
> splitting your skull with his wit . . .
> On a clear day you can see him
> plow the long fields and the lyrical English language
> along the banks of the unblue Cedar River
> This farmer knows . . .
> . . . the tensile strength of his will . . .
> he hates self-pity as he hates hate . . .
> Heart of a bull
> hand of a hawk,

ear of a dog,
eye of a cat,
James Hearst, you old Indian,
you old bastard . . .[21]

Truer scholars than I have given evidence of the tonal and topical similarities between the poems of the men. My personal attachment to the two is steeped in subjectivity from the indelible pleasure of meeting them, even in my callow state of youth. Nevertheless, their well-documented mannerisms, attentiveness to students, insatiable appetite for conversation, rural neighborliness, work-worn hands and faces, and dogged conviction that—as Hearst wrote—*fire lives on top of ashes*, make them unavoidably kindred spirits.[22]

Given the vicissitudes of the relationship, scholars have fairly questioned whether Frost and Hearst were closer than acquaintances. Although their relationship was tinged by personal hypersensitivities and agrarian envy, it was forgiving, collaborative, and ultimately fruitful. Whether there was a poor stand of alfalfa or a meager apple yield, they tilled and irrigated their friendship and stood steadfast in their mutual regard. They were "fellow bard(s)," as Frost wrote on one of his Christmas cards. They were men of idiomatic rhythms and resolve, of the rostrum and the living room, of the harness and the fickle fecundities of the earth. They were friends. As Frost once wrote, "And friends are everything. For what have we wings if not to seek friends at an elevation?"[23]

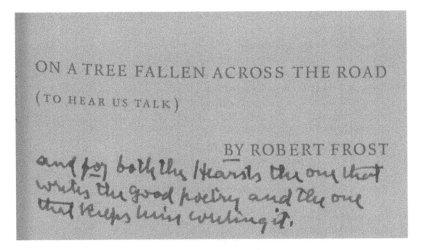

Inscription by Robert Frost to the Hearsts in his 1949 Christmas card.

WORKS CITED

Day, George. "James Hearst: Poet and Friend." https://hearstarchive.uni.edu/exhibits/james-hearst-poet-and-friend.

Engle, Paul. *Collected Poems, Prose and Plays*. Edited by Richard Poirier. New York: Library of America, 1995.

Frost, Robert. *The Collected Prose of Robert Frost*. Edited by Mark S. Richardson. Cambridge, MA: Harvard University Press, 2010.

Hass, Robert Bernard. *Going by Contraries, Robert Frost's Conflict with Science*. University Press of Virginia, 2002.

Hasselstrom, Linda M. [Interview with James Hearst]. *Sunday Clothes: A Magazine of the Fine Arts* 1, no. 1 (Spring/Summer 1972).

Hearst, James. *The Complete Poetry of James Hearst*. Edited by Scott Cawelti. Foreword by Nancy Price. Iowa City: University of Iowa Press, 2001.

———. *My Shadow Below Me*. Ames: Iowa State University Press, 1981.

———. "Roots of Poetry." *North American Review* 259, no. 3 (Fall 1974): 15–18.

Hurley, James F. "A Personal Rebuke from Robert Frost." *The Robert Frost Review*, no. 29 (2019): 9–14.

Hurley, Jim. *A Westbound Sun*. Exlibris, 2021.

Iowa, Center for the Book. "*Iowa Treasures Project/James Hearst*." State Library of Iowa.

O'Loughlin, Jim, ed. "Hearst & Frost: An Intriguing Acquaintanceship." A compilation by students, University of Northern Iowa. https://sites.google.com/uni.edu/hearstfrost/home.

———. *Planting Red Geraniums: Discovered Poems of James Hearst*. Cedar Falls: Final Thursday Press, 2017.

Sears, Jeff. "A Robert Frost of the Middlewest?" Central Michigan University, *SSML Newsletter* 19, no. 2 (1989): 18–27.

———. *The Worth of the Harvest: James Hearst and His Poetry*. Cedar Falls: Final Thursday Press, 2022.

ENDNOTES

1   Hasselstrom, *Sunday Clothes*, 40.

2   Hearst, *My Shadow Below Me*, 3. Unless otherwise noted, biographical material and direct quotes by Hearst are from his memoir *My Shadow Below Me* (1981).

3   Hearst, *My Shadow Below Me*, 6.

4   Hearst, *The Complete Poetry of James Hearst*, xxix.

5   My account of this meeting appeared in Issue 29 of the *Robert Frost Review*, "A Personal Rebuke from Robert Frost."

6   Sears, *The Worth of the Harvest*, chapter 3. This passage by Sears had been previously published in the 1989 *SSML Newsletter* essay "A Robert Frost of the Middlewest?"

7   Sears, *The Worth of the Harvest*, chapter 3.

8   It is likely that the manuscript Frost was referring to was *The Sun at Noon*, which has been described by Jeff Sears as uneven and "transitional," reflecting Hearst's desire to move away from traditional forms.

9   Sears, *The Worth of the Harvest*, chapter 3.

10   Hearst, *My Shadow Below Me*, 80–81.

11   Hearst, "Roots of Poetry," 15.

12   Hearst, *My Shadow Below Me*, 78.

13   Interview of Hearst by George Day. https://hearstarchive.uni.edu/exhibits/james-hearst-poet-and-friend.

14   From typewritten notes that Hearst made about Frost's visit to Cedar Falls. https://drive.google.com/file/d/1_5Ahpx1O7l0sh2sUFDAxbuI2sHGZhClW/view. >

15   Hearst, *My Shadow Below Me*, 82.

16   Hearst, 82.

17   Hearst, *The Collected Poetry of James Hearst*, 132; lines 4–16 of "The Visit."

18   Letter from Hearst to Frost dated July 8, 1932. Original letter preserved in the Robert Frost Collection of the Amherst College Archives. Transcribed text provided to author by Robert Hass.

19   Letter from Hearst to Kay Morrison dated April 17, 1960. Original letter preserved in the Robert Frost Collection of the Amherst College Archives. Transcribed text provided to author by Robert Bernard Hass, a coeditor of the letters of Robert Frost.

20   Originally published in 1941, the poem was reprinted and distributed for Frost's 1959 visit to the State University of Iowa. Paul Engle, "Robert Frost," in *West of Midnight* (New York: Random House, 1941), lines 1–12.

21   Published as part of a special Hearst tribute issue in the *North American Review* 259, no. 3 (1974): 12–13. The poems "Robert Frost" and "James Hearst" are reprinted with permission from the Special Collections & Archives, The University of Iowa Libraries and the copyright holder of the Engle estate. The photograph of James Hearst is reprinted with permission from the University of Northern Iowa Special Collections & University Archives.

22   Hearst, *The Collected Poetry of James Hearst*, 199; lines 10–11 of "Let's Go Inside."

23   Frost, *Collected Prose*, 130. The quotation forms the closing lines of "A Doctrine of Excursions," the preface to the 1939 work *Bread Loaf Anthology*, a collection of previously unpublished writing from the Bread Loaf Writers' Conference.

ACKNOWLEDGMENTS

The author extends grateful acknowledgment to professor Jim O'Loughlin, PhD, Department Head, College of Humanities Arts and Science, University of Northern Iowa, Cedar Falls, Iowa, for his kindness in providing research material and insights on multiple occasions, including a personal visit. Many thanks as well to the ever-responsive Emily Drennan, curator and registrar at the Hearst Center for the Arts, for her resourcefulness and referrals to Hearst scholars and archives.

"The Hand That Knows His Business":
Robert Frost, Henry David Thoreau, and the New England Work Ethic

David B. Raymond
Northern Maine Community College

Robert Frost is best known as a regional poet who renders authentic glimpses at the New England way of life through deft handling of its landscape, farms, animals, people, and speech.[1] Frost assumed a poet-farmer persona, but he was not a farmer. In fact, he came to the farm somewhat by accident and never was able to master the useful arts of the farm. As a young man, Frost was diagnosed with the early onset of tuberculosis and urged to take a job that would give him plenty of fresh air and physical activity. Impressed by a large poultry farm in Methuen, Massachusetts, he decided to try his hand at poultry farming. Staked with chickens from a local farmer and a farm in Derry, New Hampshire, paid for by his grandfather, Frost became a poultryman. Having been raised in the city, Frost knew little of farming, so he had to learn the ways of farm life by watching and working with the local farmers and farmhands. For nearly a decade, he tended chickens, cultivated orchards and gardens by day, and wrote poetry by night. This somewhat happy arrangement ended in 1906, when Frost, tired of the demands of raising hens, turned to school teaching to earn his daily bread. Even though he never returned to the farm for his livelihood, he continued to yield a bountiful harvest of material for his poetry from his farming experience.

The years spent on his farms in rural New England were crucial to Robert Frost's development as a poet and as a man. Late in life, Frost estimated that much of his poetry originated in the years spent on the Derry farm. "I've written a lot of farm poetry—country poetry— mainly because I lived in the country, knew and loved the country and farm life."[2] This practical experience chopping wood, picking apples, and mowing fields gave his poetry an authenticity that can only come from one who has done the work. Perry D. Westbrook argues that Frost's involvement with rural work was the most important factor in his "intellectual, spiritual, and artistic development."[3] Many of Frost's finest poems ("Two Tramps in Mud Time," "After Apple-Picking," and "The Death of the Hired Man") are about or include passages about work, and he is arguably "one of the few poets in the language who could make good poems out of real work", in the estimation of Jay Parini.[4] These poems do not romanticize rural work; rather, they offer an honest assessment of work and its role in the human condition. In poems like "After Apple-Picking," "A Servant to Servants," and "The Grindstone," Frost confronts straight on the pain and exhaustion that accompany work on the farm. Despite the onerous condition of labor, only a handful of Frost's poems bemoan the hardships of farm work. Most extol the virtues of work without romanticizing it. As he put it in "Mowing," "Anything more than the truth would have seemed too weak."[5]

Most critics interpret Frost's work poems as a metaphorical commentary on the craft of poetry, overlooking the philosophical implications of work described in the poem. Others have considered his work poems from the vantage point of style and technique, in particular the Georgic and pastoral style. Those who have employed these styles in the past have offered moral commentary on work and working, but this element of Frost's poetry has been overlooked or undervalued. Robert Faggen downplays the seriousness of Frost's eclogue poems, suggesting they are best read as the work of a "pastoral trickster" who is writing to "confound hierarchies of ethics and values." Matthew Parfitt takes seriously the "exhortation and moral dictum" of Frost's poems but doesn't venture an analysis of Frost's philosophy of work.[6]

While these critical approaches are useful for understanding Frost's poetics, they obscure important philosophical elements in Frost's writing. Like the New England authors he read and admired—Henry Wadsworth Longfellow, Emily Dickinson, Ralph Waldo Emerson, and Henry David Thoreau—Frost was concerned with the morality that governed the labors of his neighbors.[7] Few remember these great New England figures as philosophers of work, but most spent some of their literary capital on the subject. Longfellow through his poetry ("The Village Blacksmith," "A Psalm of Life," and "The Builders"), Emerson with his essays (his Doctrine of the Farm in "Man the Reformer"), and Thoreau through his most famous book (*Walden, or Life in the Woods*) all testify to their concern and consideration on the subject.

Recent studies have established the influence of Thoreau on several of Frost's work poems. Justine Pojanowski-Todd, in her analysis of "The Death of the Hired Man," finds "a distinctly political Frost, one whose footing in Thoreauvian ideas about individualism and self-reliance intersects with his views on the moral implications of work and the threat of profit-driven industry on the rural character of New England."[8] George Monteiro, in his study *Robert Frost & the New England Renaissance*, shows the resemblance between Frost's French Canadian woodsman Baptiste in "The Ax-Helve" and Thoreau's chopper Alex Therien in *Walden*. Later in the same book, Monterio establishes a connection between the work values found in "Two Tramps in Mud Time, or a Full-time Interest," and those expressed by Thoreau in *Walden* and "Life without Principle."[9] These limited studies suggest the two men may have shared a common moral ground on work. Given Frost's admiration for *Walden*, it seems likely that other work poems will bear the imprint of Thoreau's philosophical musings about work as well.

At first glance, Thoreau seems an unlikely philosopher of work.[10] By reputation and deed, he was not known as an industrious man. He never held a steady job, never worked more than a few weeks out of every year. However, a close reading of *Walden* and "Life without Principle" proves him to be one of the most astute and insightful commentators on work in the history of American culture. His wisdom about work began with his lifelong pursuit of self-culture or character development.[11] To cultivate his soul, Thoreau read, reflected, and wrote about the art of living. For most of his life, he struggled to find work that satisfied his talents and dovetailed with his self-culture. At first, he thought simplifying his material wants to work less would solve the problem, but he quickly realized that it was not enough to work less. He needed work that was pleasurable for if getting a living is not inviting and glorious then living would not be (LwP 637).[12] Self-culture meant that his work would be subject to the higher laws of morality. He was adamant that there was an honest way to work that entailed not just forthrightness in the marketplace but also integrity in the way one worked and the product or services provided. Each task has an ideal that can be used to judge whether a job is done right, and Thoreau held it immoral to do a job that was not up to the highest standard of that trade or profession. In time, he concluded that those who do work they love will do it well because they find the act of work pleasurable when done by the standards of the task.

The broad contours of Thoreau's philosophy of work can be found in the philosophical musings found in Frost's work poetry. Among his many poems, two are foundational to understanding his philosophy of work. The first, "The Code—Heroics," lays out succinctly the basic moral guidelines for work in two lines: "The hand that knows his business won't be told / To do work better or faster—those two things." A rural man always works hard and to the best of his ability. Those who worked by the Code found dignity and worth in what they did for a living and respect from the community for the way that they did their work. Following "The Code" in time but not importance is Frost's oft-anthologized poem "Two Tramps in Mud Time, or a Full-time Interest." This piece is a poetic rendering of the Code in action and a meditation on the importance of doing work that you love for a living. In this poem, Frost links the love of work to the quality just as Thoreau did.

Reginald Cook sees Frost and Thoreau as "parallel parabalists" who seek to impart wisdom to their readers. Frost defined a parable as "a story that means what it says and something besides." Thoreau, the philosopher-poet, began with an idea, contemplated its implications, then sought the application and validation of the principle through practical experience. Frost was more of a poet-philosopher who gained insight by working alongside farmers, observing their ways, and reflecting on the experience before committing his insight to verse.[13] Despite their differences in approach, the two men develop strikingly similar philosophies of work. They embrace the same vision of the morality of work, the importance of pleasure in work, and the strong connection between the two. They also recognize that work done by a moral code gives the worker a sense of dignity and worth as a human being. Given Frost's admiration for the writings of Thoreau, especially *Walden*, it seems plausible that the "something besides" that Frost put into his work poems would be shaped by Thoreau's philosophy of work. The purpose of this paper is to trace the contours of Frost's philosophy of work and compare it to that of Thoreau. Such an analysis will show that Frost's views are strikingly similar to Thoreau's.

The Code: Work Better or Faster

In many ways the work ethic of Frost and Thoreau was gleaned from the lives of the farmers of Concord and Derry. The roots of the New England work ethic go deep into the history of the region. The Puritan settlers brought a "balanced social ethic combining hard work, temperate living, civic virtue, and spiritual devotion" to the New World.[14] Work was viewed as a call from God to labor at a divinely ordained task, most likely farming. Exercising one's God-given talent and working hard brought glory to God and led to the production of quality goods and services that contributed to the common good. Work was also a discipline that served as a deterrent to sin, for those who were busy were not as susceptible to the devil's temptations. Those who worked diligently and lived a godly life would be rewarded by God, if not in the present life then certainly in the life to come. Those who shirked their duties and lived a sinful life would be punished. In short, dedication to one's God-given vocation invested work with a moral significance beyond the economic transaction.

As time moved on, the religious foundation of the New England work ethic eroded and work lost its divine mandate to pursue God's calling and work for His glory. Individuals still believed they labored for the greater good, but now the greater good was defined by an enlightened pursuit of self-interest through the efficient production of goods and services, not by self-denial and sacrifice for God and the good of others. The more useful one became, the more profit one would make. Idleness was deplored not as a gateway to sin but as a lost opportunity to make money. Shorn of its religious and moral trappings, work became little more than a way to wealth. Despite the shifting climate surrounding the work ethic, some of the mandates of the Puritan work ethic—find your calling; do it well for your well-being and the benefit of others—remained constant over time and were embraced by both Frost and Thoreau. In some ways, both men felt a sense of calling on their work as writers. Thoreau insisted he was following his genius in pursuit of truth and wisdom through his work as a writer, but Frost harbored a sense of calling much like the early Puritans. He believed each person had a calling from God and that pursuing that calling helped to fulfill the purpose God gave to each person. Those who did achieved "self-respect and the approval of God and society."[15]

The moral significance of work occurs in one of Frost's early poems, "The Code—Heroics" (1914). This narrative poem is a story within a story, both of which take place during haying season. In the early 1900s, gathering hay involved two men: one on the ground pitching hay onto the wagon, and another on the wagon skillfully piling the hay to maximize the size of the load and ensure its stability for transport from the field to the barn. Upon return to the farm, the wagon was moved into the barn, and the hay was unloaded by lifting it into the mow (upper level of a barn) or by dumping it down into the bay. As the poem opens, three men are gathering hay in an open field. James, one of two farmhands, walks off the field after mulling over the observation of the "town-bred farmer" about the impending rainstorm. Taking the farmer's comment as a veiled complaint about the pace of the farmhands' work, James is insulted and walks off. Perplexed, the town-bred farmer asks the remaining farmhand what was wrong. The farmhand explains that the farmer does not know the ways of rural men and he explains the essence of the Code that they lived by: "The hand that knows his business won't be told / To do work better or faster—those two things."

It is unclear what it means to work "faster," but one can get a sense of the pace of work by comparing the concept in Frost's other work poems. It is not the pace set by Sanders, who is a vital figure in the second story, to whom "(d)aylight and lantern-light were one" when it came to work. At first glance, this line sounds like high praise for a man who worked in heroic proportions, but his penchant for hard work had a dark side. Sanders loved to "bull" his crew by working behind a row of mowers, cutting close to their heels to force them to work faster. If this "encouragement" had come from a peer, it would have been viewed as a friendly challenge to see who could work faster. However, since it came from the employer, it was deemed a selfish attempt to "drive" the crew like beasts of burden to extract the maximum labor without regard for the workers' well-being. Sanders might be admired as a hard worker, but he was despised for his inhumane treatment of his farmhands.

At the other extreme is Silas, the prodigal farmhand in "The Death of the Hired Hand." Warren condemns Silas for leaving during the middle of haying season to take a job that promised more money. He does not begrudge Silas a chance to better himself, but Silas does not remain with his new job either. What most troubles Warren is Silas's failure to work steadily until the job is done. Hay reaches its peak growth in late summer, and once it is cut, there is a limited time to gather it into the barn. Leave wet hay in the field too long, and it molds; put it in the barn too soon, and it becomes combustible. Once the hay "makes," the crew must work steadily at the task until it is done. Like the faithless hired hands in "A Servant to Servants" who could not be counted on to work when the boss was not around, Silas was unreliable when his labor was needed most.

Between the excess of Sanders and the deficiency of Silas is the golden mean of hard work. Steady work is more productive than relentless labor, as the veteran farmhand Pike explains to his young associate Dick in "From Plane to Plane." In this poem, the two men are hoeing a field. When they reach the end of the row, they walk back to where they started at the head of the field before hoeing again. When Dick asks his seasoned partner why he does not hoe both ways, Pike claims hoeing both ways would exhaust the worker. The rest afforded by the short walk back to the starting point makes the worker more productive. Hard work is not incessant without rest, nor is it slow and unproductive. Hard work is a measured pace, steady and rhythmic, like swinging an axe as described in "Two Tramps in Mud Time," that moves the work forward until the task is finished without exhausting the worker.

Work must not only be done at a steady, measured pace; it must also be done well. Again, Frost does not offer a precise definition of quality work. Rather, he assumes his readers will recognize good work when they "see" it through description and imagery. Walter Jost reminds us that we need to pay close attention to "what the poem is *doing*" to understand the meaning of Frost's poems.[16] In "The Code," the farmhand's skill at building a load of hay is revealed at the climax of the poem when the hired hand tries to bury Sanders under the hay. There is an art to piling hay on a wagon so that as much hay as possible can be transported from the field to the barn without losing any in transit. Piled well, the hay can be unloaded quickly and efficiently. When challenged by Sanders to work faster, the narrator is able to dump the whole "rackful on him in ten lots." Only one skilled in building a load of hay could find the piling points that made for quick and easy unloading of the wagon in his attempt to bury Sanders.

Quality is crucial to understanding "The Grindstone." In this poem, two men are working in tandem to sharpen a scythe. The younger man is pumping the grinding wheel while the older man holds the scythe edge to the wheel. It is a slow, laborious process. The narrator, exhausted from pumping the grinding wheel, returning "hate for hate" with the wheel, wants to give up grinding, "leaving something to the whetter" (a whetstone is used by a mower to sharpen his scythe in the field), but the "Father-Time-like man" quietly goes about his business sharpening the scythe, examining it with the "disinterested" eye of one who knew by sight the look of a well-honed blade. Unlike the young narrator, who was willing to quit once the sharpness of the blade was close enough, the old man "knows his business" and will not leave off until the job is "all that it should be."

Other poems are more precise in their imagery. In "Two Tramps in Mud Time," the narrator is hard at work chopping large blocks of oak, a hardwood notoriously difficult to split, and is wielding his axe adroitly. Should the axe not strike true, the pieces will splinter endlessly, posing a danger to the hands of all who dare to handle it. Since every piece "fell splinterless as a cloven rock," it is clear that the hand that wields the axe knows his business. Likewise, in "The Ax-Helve" the reader knows the quality of the ax-helves made by Baptiste through Frost's description. The kind of wood used (hickory), the way the handle was fashioned with the grain for strength, and the way it was cut to the right thickness to allow it to bend but not break are all characteristics of a well-made handle.

Doing quality work was a moral mandate for Thoreau as well. He believed all of life, including work, is governed by the higher laws of morality and he strove to work as he lived. "The aim of the laborer should be, not to get his living, to get 'a good job,' but to perform well a certain work and, even in a pecuniary sense, it would be economy for a town to pay its laborers so well that they would not feel that they were working for low ends, as for a livelihood merely, but for scientific, or even moral ends" (LwP 635). In Thoreau's mind, poor quality work is as dishonest as inaccurate measurements or unjust prices. Those who shortcut quality usually do so to lessen costs and increase profits. The man who loves his work will always do a better job because he enjoys and respects his work; he will never violate the integrity or ideal of the work.

Thoreau firmly believed all work should be conceived and completed as a craftsman or artist conceives his or her work: it must be done for the sake of the craft not merely for money. He illustrates his point with a fable about the artist of Kouroo. The artist was employed to make a simple staff, but he desires to make the perfect staff, using only the best material and doing the work with the greatest of skill and technique. He becomes so engrossed in his work, he loses track of time. Years passed without notice until he emerges from his shop with an ideal staff of "full and fair proportions." Thoreau concludes that if we undertake our work with a "singleness of purpose and resolution," striving for perfection, we will perform well our work (*Walden* 565–66).

A practical example of this principle is found in Thoreau's construction of the chimney for his cabin. When he built the chimney, he approached it like the artist of Kouroo. First, he studied the art of masonry so that he could do the job right. Knowing that a fireplace is the vital center of any dwelling, he "lingered" about the task, taking his time to carefully design the front of the fireplace. Work proceeded slowly but accurately, rising "square and solid by degrees." Once complete, it served not only as a source of heat and warmth but also a source of pride for it was a job well done. "I had got a couple of old fire-logs to keep the wood from the hearth, and it did me good to see the soot form on the back of the chimney which I had built, and I poked the fire with more right and more satisfaction than usual" (487). His concern for the quality of work led him to conclude that good work takes time. Work too fast and quality will suffer; work too slow and the needful tasks of seasonal farm labor will not get done in time. Seeds won't get planted, weeds will overtake the crops, animals will go hungry, and wood will not be laid up for winter.

Likewise, the pace of work was a matter of concern to Thoreau. In *Walden* Thoreau laments his neighbors who were driving themselves like an overseer on a Southern plantation or putting the twelve labors of Hercules to shame with their efforts (*Walden* 260, 263). Since Thoreau was not driven by mammonism like his neighbors, he was able to limit his work and approach to it in a manner that resembled the sauntering way he took his daily walk. Sauntering is a steady, unhurried pace that allows the walker to take in the beauty and spiritual reality of nature ("Walking," 592–95). The same pace suited those who wanted to perform well a certain task. When describing his work on the cabin at Walden Pond in April, he wrote, "I made no haste in my work, but rather made the most of it." There was plenty of time to build the cabin and he was determined to take his time and do it well. Thoreau's model for the appropriate pace was the French Canadian woodchopper who was never in a hurry to do his work, always taking careful consideration of the best way to do his job well (*Walden* 297, 394–97).

Not if He Values What He Is: Dignity

Driving the conflicts in "The Code" is a sense of dignity that accrued to the worker if he lived and worked by the ideals of the Code. The hand that knows his business won't be told to work faster or better without rising to defend his integrity as a worker and as a man. Dignity was crucial for the well-being of New Englanders, who often struggled to cobble together a living in the region's harsh environment. Frost was impressed with the quiet dignity of the denizens of the rural regions north of Boston, and he took his stand with them against a "decadent, lost society."[17] This explains why some of Frost's characters fiercely defended their honor against anyone who questioned their commitment to the Code. Critics have written off the confrontations in "The Code" as humorous incidents not to be taken seriously, manifestations of class antagonisms, or deadly serious confrontations that expose the barbarity of rural farm laborers.[18] There is some truth in these assessments, but viewed in light of the moral mandates of the Code, the conflicts seem to hinge more on the worker's dignity than these other matters.

The two conflicts in "The Code," are the direct result of a challenge to the farmhand's fidelity to the Code and hence to his integrity as a man. In both stories, the farmhands took offense when their pace of work was questioned by the farmers. In the first case, James mistook the town-bred farmer's comments about rain as an implied criticism of the pace of his work. The second story involved a long-standing grudge between Sanders and the unnamed farmhand. Sanders was notorious for his demanding work ethic and for pushing his crew beyond the reasonable boundaries of hard work set forth by the Code. Sanders's bullying persisted until one summer afternoon when the farmhand was "paired up" with Sanders to bring in the hay. Sanders was on the ground pitching hay onto the wagon and the narrator was on the load piling hay as it was pitched onto the wagon. Once the two finished the load and returned to the barn, Sanders jumped down into the bay and "shouts like a captain" to the hired hand, "Let her come!," a common competitive challenge issued by rural men to each other to see who could work the fastest. On this day, the narrator is on the wagon, pitching hay off the load and downward to Sanders. This puts him at a decided advantage over Sanders who must exert significantly more effort to move the hay pitched down to him into piles in the lower region of the barn. The hired man knows he is in a position to "bull" Sanders, so he asks him to repeat his command. Sanders, prideful of his work ethic and unwilling to back down, repeats the challenge, albeit "softer" the second time. "Never you say a thing like that to a man, / Not if he values what he is . . ." the farmhand explains. The farmhand starts slowly, then dumps the whole load on Sanders in ten lots, burying him under the hay. Or so he thought. When another crew arrived to unload their hay, they sensed what the hired hand had done and frantically pitched hay out into the barn floor to rescue Sanders, but Sanders did not need rescuing. He had escaped the onslaught of hay and retreated to the house where he remained to avoid facing the hired man who had "hurt his dignity" by outworking him. When the "town-bred farmer" asked if Sanders fired him for trying to bury him in the hay, the hired man replied, "Discharge me? No! He knew I did just right." Sanders lived by the Code as much as the farmhand did and he recognized that his challenge to work faster had been met and he had been bested by the farmhand. Firing his hired hand under these circumstances would have been unthinkable, for it would have been an admission of defeat that would have further damaged Sanders' dignity.

Dignity plays an important part in several other work poems. Dignity helps to explain Pike's defiant claim that he would not hoe "both ways for anybody" in "From Plane to Plane." Earlier in the poem, he claimed he wouldn't hoe both ways so he could increase productivity or give the weeds a truce, but these comments mask the real reason for not hoeing both ways: dignity. Hoeing both ways deprives the worker of a brief respite from his physical labor. No human being should be subjected to unrelenting work. "Everyone has to keep his extrication," Pike explains, to keep from "getting bogged down / In what he has to do to earn a living." Dignity is also central to Warren and Mary's debate over what to do with Silas in the "The Death of the Hired Man." When Silas threatened to leave Warren for higher pay elsewhere, Warren warned him that he would not have him back if he left. Silas left anyway. Now in his time of need, Silas returns to the farm with a plan to clear the upper pasture and teach the Wilson boy how to build a load of hay. Mary sides with Silas reminding Warren that Silas is skilled at building a load of hay. "Surely you wouldn't grudge the poor old man

/ Some humble way to save his self-respect," Mary pleads, but Warren will have none of it. He justifies his coldness by reminding Mary that Silas has a brother who could help, but Mary again takes pity on Silas and wants to spare his pride and dignity. "Worthless though he is," Mary argues, he should not "be made ashamed" to beg his brother for help, but Warren is unmoved. Only the death of Silas resolves the debate over his worth as a worker and dignity as a man.

Dignity concerned Thoreau in the same manner that it troubled Frost. In *Walden*, Thoreau railed against the new mode of work brought on by the Market Revolution that made men into machine tenders, depriving them of joy in their work and robbing them of their dignity as men. He found it detestable that some people were able, through wealth and power, to live off the labor of others. In various passages, Thoreau condemns the factory that operated not that men might have goods more cheaply and abundantly but that corporations might be enriched, railed against the railroads that exploited Irish labor to construct tracks, and condemned Southern plantation owners who lived off the labor of their slaves whom they treated as chattel property. Under these forms of labor, the workers were robbed of their dignity as human beings. Artisans and farmers had greater freedom, but still could not "afford to sustain the manliest relations to men" for their "labor would be depreciated in the marketplace." Dependent on trade in the marketplace for their livelihood, they end up "lying, flattering, voting, contracting (them)selves into a nutshell of civility, or dilating into an atmosphere of thin and vaporous generosity" in order to persuade their neighbor to let them "make his shoes, or his hat, or his coat, or his carriage, or import his groceries for him." They do not have "leisure for a true integrity day by day," There is "no time to be anything but a machine" (*Walden*, 261–62, 289–90, 311, 345).

Only Where Love and Need Are One

The other foundational poem that helps to explain Frost's philosophy of work is "Two Tramps in Mud Time, or a Full-time Interest" (1934). Whereas "The Code" laid down the moral standards for doing work well and established the relationship between the Code and the dignity of the worker, "Two Tramps in Mud Time," offers a portrait of the Code in action and a philosophical musing on the relationship between loving work and doing it well. As with most of

Frost's work poems, many critics have followed the well-worn path of interpretation that reads these poems as a commentary on the craft of poetry. Others have read the poem as a philosophical defense of the individual's rights against those of the community or as a conservative critique of New Deal liberalism.[19] Few have read the poem in light of the insight that it sheds on the role of work in the lives of rural New Englanders.

The poem opens with a man chopping firewood in a woodlot when two tramps (lumberjacks) come out of the woods and hint for work by greeting the narrator with a call to "Hit them hard." The tramps linger to watch the narrator at work, gauging whether he knew how to handle an axe, for if he didn't, they hoped to take his work for pay. The second stanza makes clear that the narrator is a hand that knows his business as narrator strikes the block of wood with precision, splitting the wood into splinterless chunks. As the poem progresses, the narrator ponders "what they came to ask." He realizes that he does the work not just for firewood, but because he loves his task. He enjoys the skill of chopping, the physical demands of the work, and savors the experience of working in harmony with nature. The narrator works in a steady, measured pace, swinging the axe in a rhythmic way that ensures the accuracy of each blow. Through Frost's vivid and animated description, one can almost feel the pleasure and rhythm of swinging an axe and chopping the wood. "The weight of an ax-head poised aloft, / The grip on earth of outspread feet, / The life of muscles rocking soft / And smooth and moist in vernal heat." Even the sound of these lines gives the reader a feel for the rhythmic motion used in the chopping of firewood.

Then there is the joy of working in harmony with nature. The description of nature in stanzas three through five has been deemed irrelevant by one critic, but these lines are essential to the message of the poem.[20] Part of the pleasure of chopping wood is time spent in the woods, not simply soaking in its beauty but being one with nature. The narrator is enjoying the beauty of a spring day, hearing the bluebird, feeling the warmth of the sun that hints at better spring days ahead, and the chill of an April breeze that reminds him that he is temporally situated between winter and summer. Only one who has spent many hours in the woods can speak with such beauty and accuracy.

Had Frost ended his "Two Tramps in Mud Time" in the sixth stanza, it would have stood as an exquisite expression of the Code in action, but Frost presses his chopping ode to its logical conclusion. Having established the pleasure of work, the narrator returns to the moral dilemma introduced in the first stanza to ponder anew the request of the tramps to take his work for pay. Does he have any right to work for play when these tramps wanted to work for need? At first, he admits, "My right might be love, but theirs was need. / And where the two exist in twain / Thiers was the better right—agreed," but then concludes the question is wrongly framed. It is not enough to work out of need; one must work for love too. Refusing to yield to the separation, he is determined to unite his avocation and vocation as his "two eyes make one in sight." Frost then comes to the epiphany that only those who love their work and abide by the Code (heaven's sake), will do it well. "Only where love and need are one, / And work is play for mortal stakes / Is the deed ever really done / For Heaven and the future's sakes."

The epiphany of the final stanza expresses in poetic form Thoreau's belief that good work is always done by those who do it for the love of it and not simply for the money. Thoreau believed that those who love their work will do it well. It was not enough to "get your living by loving" (LwP 636). Rather, the "aim of the laborer should be, not to get his living, to get 'a good job,'" "but to perform well a certain work" (LwP 635). Later in life, when Thoreau turned to surveying to earn his living, he learned that those who master a craft get pleasure from exercising their skills and abilities. The work of a surveyor was well suited to Thoreau's natural gifts and abilities. It allowed him to spend time in nature (a valuable experience for Transcendentalists), to exercise his natural propensity and skills for measurement, while providing a valuable service to the community. This led him to the logical conclusion that the way to get pleasure from work is to find work you love and master the skills required to do the work well. This is why he cautioned his readers to "not hire a man who does your work for money, but him who does it for the love of it" (LwP 635). Loving work leads to quality while loving money does not.

Both men found that working for the necessities of life (food, clothing, shelter, and fuel) was innately satisfying as well. Frost learned from experience that working to provide needs, like firewood, was pleasurable to the worker. It is the love of farming that gives one "passion for the earth" and "burns through the Putting in the Seed / on through the watching for that early birth" ("Putting in the Seed").

Likewise, in "Mowing" where the narrator expresses his "earnest love" of laying the hay out in rows.[21] Love was the reason Baptiste could "make a short job long / For love of it, and yet not waste time either," the art of working better and faster captured in two artful lines ("The Axe-Helve"). Loving work is eloquently expressed by Mary in her defense of Silas in "The Death of the Hired Man." Work done out of love gives the worker "something to look backward to with pride" and something to "look forward to with hope."

Likewise, Thoreau found pleasure in working for his basic needs. Throughout *Walden*, there are numerous examples of the pleasure he derived from doing the simple tasks of growing his food, building his cabin, cutting his firewood, and tending his bean field.[22] During his first summer at Walden, Thoreau built his cabin and learned that constructing one's shelter connects the builder to his building (*Walden* 300). He found a similar attachment to his woodpile. A squarely stacked cord of wood, piled with sweat and pain, awaiting the warm reward of a wood fire in the middle of the winter is both a necessity and a pleasure. "Every man looks at his woodpile with a kind of affection," Thoreau wrote, "I love to have mine before my window, and the more chips, the better to remind me of my pleasing work" (*Walden* 496). Even the two and a half acres of beans he planted for the market were a joy to Thoreau. By using hand tools rather than horse-drawn implements, Thoreau becomes "intimate" with his beans. Over the summer, he "came to love (his) rows," hoeing each morning diligently, chasing off woodchucks and squirrels, and keeping a constant vigil against the beans' mortal enemy, the weed (*Walden* 404–16).[23]

Conclusion

In the end, it is clear that Frost and Thoreau shared a common vision of good work. One of Frost's earliest poems, "The Tuft of Flowers" conveys the "spirit kindred" that binds rural men together through their work. At the poem's beginning, the narrator goes to a field to rake freshly mowed hay, turning it over to the sun to dry. As he enters the field, he looks in vain for the one who mowed the grass. Unable to find him, the narrator concludes that most work is of a solitary nature. The mower and the raker seem to work in separate spheres with no connection to each other. Then his gaze is diverted by a butterfly flitting about the field, eventually drawing his attention to a tuft of flowers left by the mower. Realizing the mower intentionally skipped over the flowers out of respect for the beauty of nature, the narrator suddenly feels a connection to the one who went before him. By the end of the poem, the narrator no longer feels isolated because he now realizes men are bound together by their shared work values "whether they work together or apart."

Frost experienced the Code through the "fellowship of labor," to borrow a phrase from Carl Van Doren,[24] as he worked alongside the local farmers of the region. For generations, New Englanders had passed on the Code by deed and example. Frost took in these lessons as generations of New Englanders who came before him had, by watching and working with others in the fields and forests learning by example. What he felt there must have been made clear by his reading *Walden* and other works by Thoreau, for Thoreau had thought long and hard about the way to make a living by and "honest and agreeable manner" (*Walden* 308). Thoreau, too, found validation for his thoughts in the work and lives of the small farmers and craftsmen of Concord. George Minott, Reuben Rice, George Melvin, Sam Barrett, Cyrus Hubbard, and others were men highly esteemed by Thoreau because they exemplified with their lives, and not just their words, the simple life he sought to live. These were men of quiet, stoical integrity who subjected their lives to the higher laws of morality. From these encounters, Frost and Thoreau took in an ethic of work that was as old as New England itself.

Frost likely would have arrived at the same rendition of the Code by experience and observation, but his familiarity with the writings of Thoreau steadied his hand as he penned his poems. Both men believed that one should work steadily and well at a task of one's choosing to provide quality goods and services that benefited society and gave dignity to the worker. The key to this kind of work was doing work that you loved, for those who love their work will instinctively do it by the Code. This was the "work wisdom" of Walden Pond and of Derry farm.

WORKS CITED

Andrews, Barry M. *Transcendentalism and the Cultivation of the Soul.* Amherst: University of Massachusetts, 2018.

Applebaum, Herbert A. *The American Work Ethic and the Changing Work Force: An Historical Perspective.* Westport, CT: Greenwood Publishing Group, 1998.

———. *The Concept of Work: Ancient, Medieval, and Modern.* Albany: State University of New York Press, 1992.

Barron, Jonathan N. *How Robert Frost Made Realism Matter.* Columbia: University of Missouri Press, 2016.

Bernstein, Paul. *American Work Values.* Albany: State University of New York Press, 1997.

Borroff, Marie. "Robert Frost: 'To Earthward.'" In *Frost Centennial Essays II*, edited by Jac Tharpe, 21–39. Jackson: University Press of Mississippi, 1976.

Buell, Lawrence. "Frost as a New England Poet." In *The Cambridge Companion to Robert Frost*, edited by Robert Faggen, 101–22. Cambridge: Cambridge University Press, 2001.

Cafaro, Philip. *Thoreau's Living Ethics: Walden and the Pursuit of Virtue.* Athens: University of Georgia Press, 2004.

Carruth, Hayden. *Selected Essays and Reviews.* Port Townsend, WA: Copper Canyon Press, 1996.

Cook, Reginald L. "A Parallel of Parablists: Thoreau and Frost." In *The Thoreau Centennial*, edited by Walter Harding, 65–79. Albany: State University of New York Press, 1964.

Faggen, Robert. "Frost and the Question of the Pastoral." In *The Cambridge Companion to Robert Frost*, edited by Robert Faggen, 49–74. Cambridge: Cambridge University Press, 2001.

———. *Robert Frost and the Challenge of Darwin.* Ann Arbor: University of Michigan Press, 1997.

Feaster, John. "Robert Frost's 'The Code': A Context and Commentary." *Cresset* 55, no. 7 (1992): 6–10.

Frost, Robert. *Collected Poems, Prose, & Plays.* Edited by Richard Poirier and Mark Richardson. New York: Library of America, 1995.

———. "What Became of New England?" In *Robert Frost: Poetry and Prose*, edited by Edward Connery Lathem and Lawrance Thompson, 385–96. New York: Holt, Rinehart and Winston, 1972.

Hoffman, Tyler B. "Robert Frost and the Politics of Labor." *Modern Language Studies* 29, no. 2 (Autumn, 1999): 109–35.

Jost, Walter. "'The Lurking Frost': Poetic and Rhetoric in 'Two Tramps in Mud Time.'" *American Literature* 60, no. 2 (May 1988): 226–40.

Kearns, Katherine. *Robert Frost and a Poetics of Appetite.* Cambridge: Cambridge University Press, 1994.

Kemp, John C. *Robert Frost and New England: The Poet as Regionalist.* Princeton, NJ: Princeton University Press, 1979.

Mertens, Louis. *Robert Frost: Life and Talks-Walking.* Norman: University of Oklahoma Press, 1965.

Monteiro, George. "Frost's Hired Hand." *College Literature* 14, no. 2 (Spring 1987): 128–135.

———. *Robert Frost & the New England Renaissance.* Louisville: University Press of Kentucky, 1988.

Parfitt, Matthew. "Robert Frost's 'Modern Georgics.'" *The Robert Frost Review*, no. 6 (Fall 1996): 54–70.

Parini, Jay. *Robert Frost: A Life.* New York: Henry Holt and Company, 1999.

Perrine, Laurence. "'Two Tramps in Mud Time' and the Critics." *American Literature* 44, no. 4 (1973): 671–76.

Poirier, Richard. *Robert Frost: The Work of Knowing.* Stanford, CA: Stanford University Press, 1977.

Pojanowski-Todd, Justine. "The Commercial Spirit and a Changing New England: Thoreau's Philosophy of Work in Frost's 'Death of the Hired Man.'" *The Robert Frost Review*, no. 30 (2021): 15–28.

Raymond, David B. "Henry David Thoreau and the American Work Ethic." *The Concord Saunterer: A Journal of Thoreau Studies*. New Series Volume 17 (2009): 137–156.

———. "Thoreau's 'Life without Principle' and the Art of Living and Getting a Living." *Philosophy and Literature* 45, no. 2 (2021): 397–415.

Rodgers, Daniel T. *The Work Ethic in Industrial America, 1850–1920*. Chicago: University of Chicago Press, 1979 paperback edition of 1974.

Shi, David E. *The Simple Life: Plain Living and High Thinking in American Culture*. Athens: University of Georgia Press, 2001.

Thoreau, Henry David. *The Journal of Henry D. Thoreau*. Edited by Bradford Torrey and Francis H. Allen. New York: Dover Publications, Inc., 1962 reprint of 1906 edition.

———. *The Portable Thoreau*. Edited by Carl Bode. New York: Penguin Books, 1977.

Van Doren, Carl. *Many Minds*. New York: Alfred A. Knopf, 1924.

Westbrook, Perry D. "Robert Frost's New England." In *Frost Centennial Essays*, edited by Jac Tharpe, 239–55. Jackson: University of Mississippi, 1974.

ENDNOTES

1   Kemp, *Robert Frost and New England*, 97–104.

2   Quoted in Mertens, *Robert Frost*, 310, 399.

3   Westbrook, "Robert Frost's New England," 239–55.

4   Parini, *Robert Frost*, 78.

5   All references to Frost poems are from *Complete Poems, Prose & Plays*.

6   Faggen, "Frost and the Question of the Pastoral," 49–74; Parfitt, "Robert Frost's Modern Georgics," 54–70. One problem with Parfitt's interpretation is his denigration of the ethical principles that undergird rural work. If Georgics extol the ethical principles of work, then the critic must take seriously the work ethic of rural New Englanders.

7   For an analysis of the influence of New England authors on Frost, see Buell, "Frost as a New England Poet," 101–22.

8   Pojanowski-Todd, "The Commercial Spirit and a Changing New England," 15–28.

9   Monteiro, *Robert Frost & the New England Renaissance*, 57–65 and 76–81.

10   For an overview of Thoreau's thinking on work, see Cafaro, *Thoreau's Living Ethics*, 97–103; Raymond, "Henry David Thoreau and the American Work Ethic," 137–56; and "Thoreau's 'Life without Principle' and the Art of Living and Getting a Living," 397–415.

11   For a brief introduction to self-culture, see Andrews, *Transcendentalism and the Cultivation of the Soul*, and Cafaro, *Thoreau's Living Ethics*, 16–44.

12   All references to *Walden* and "Life without Principle" are from *The Portable Thoreau*, abbreviated as *Walden* and LwP in the in-text citations.

13   For an interesting study of the similar approach of Frost and Thoreau, see Cook, "A Parallel of Parablists," 65–79.

14   Shi, *The Simple Life*, 8–15. For an overview of the Puritan work ethic, see Bernstein, *American Work Values*, 69–99. For more on the work ethic, see Rodgers, *The Work Ethic in Industrial America, 1850–1920*, 7–14; and Applebaum, *The American Work Ethic and the Changing Work Force*, 63–81. For a broad overview of the history of the work ethic, see Applebaum, *The Concept of Work*.

15 Westbrook, "Robert Frost's New England," 250.

16 Jost, "'The Lurking Frost'; Poetic and Rhetoric in 'Two Tramps in Mud Time,'" 226–40.

17 Frost, "What Became of New England?," 385–89.

18 Critics who write off this poem as humorous should heed Frost's caution to his readers that he is never so serious as when he was being funny. See Faggen, "Frost and the Question of the Pastoral," 54 and Westbrook, "Robert Frost's New England," 250–51. In his study of Frost and Darwinism, Faggen reads the poem bleakly as a tale of class antagonism and resentment with hatred and violence bubbling just below the surface of employer-employee relations; see Faggen, *Robert Frost and the Challenge of Darwin*, 132–35. See also Feaster, "Robert Frost's 'The Code': A Context and a Commentary," 6–10. Those who read the conflicts as violent episodes of rural barbarity, see Barron, *How Robert Frost Made Realism Matter*, 205–208; Kemp, *Robert Frost and New England*, 128; Parfitt, "Robert Frost's 'Modern Georgics,'" 63; Faggen, "Frost and the Question of the Pastoral," 54. Monteiro rightly asserts that the two hired hands knew their business and wanted respect for their prowess, but he, too, errs on the side of violence as the usual response to offense. See Monteiro, "Frost's Hired Hand," 132–34.

19 Laurence Perrine summarizes the literature best in "'Two Tramps in Mud Time' and the Critics," 671–76. As mentioned previously, George Monteiro points out common ideals in both the poem and the works of Thoreau but fails to recognize it as a poetic statement of the blessings and pleasure that come from doing work that you love and doing it well.

20 Hayden Carruth deems these stanzas unnecessary but viewed from the vantage point of work; they are essential to the narrator's pleasure with his work. See Carruth, *Selected Essays and Reviews*, 156.

21 In his reading of "Mowing," Richard Poirier argues that pleasure comes solely from the act of work, not the product the mower has no control over. In a limited way, this is true, but the wise farmer knows when the hay is ready, the time of day to cut it, and the length of time it needs to make. In this way, the farmer does exert a degree of control over the results. See Poirier, *Robert Frost*, 288.

22 Marie Borroff points in this direction but does not probe the matter too deeply when she writes that Frost often wrote of the love of work that comes from the physical pleasure (and pain) from our contact with the world. She contends, "It follows that work, in that it is a form of willed encounter between body and world, is also, for Frost, a form of love." See Borroff, "Robert Frost," 25.

23 Richard Poirier questions whether anyone can "know" beans. Perhaps he is overthinking the metaphor of "knowing" one's beans or maybe he lacks the practical experience of farming. See Poirier, *Robert Frost*, 278.

24 Van Doren, *Many Minds*, 63.

(Be)wildered and Rewildered by Robert Frost's "The Tuft of Flowers"

Matthew Teorey
Peninsula College

A number of scholars take for granted that "The Tuft of Flowers" and other Robert Frost poems about rural New England champion a traditional, stable, simple, orderly country temperament as sanctuary from a modern, uncertain, complex, chaotic city temperament. Robert Hass, for example, asserts Frost's poems favor "a common belief that country life offers a safe refuge" from the uncertainties of urban life.[1] Laborers in these pastorals surpass city dwellers by successfully resisting "the debased life of mass culture" because they "become more attuned to the rhythms of nature and take great satisfaction in wresting order from chaos as they cultivate the soil."[2] Robert Faggen adds that Frost's nature poetry "depicts retreat . . . from universal chaos"[3] pervading modern society. John Cooper comments on a flaw in this analysis, pointing out that the "isolated, dismayed, bewildered"[4] ethos of modern urban life had already infiltrated rural spaces by Frost's day, so it is unlikely he adopted the "Virgilian poetics of retreat into the countryside as the domain of simple pleasures and honest values." However, the claim that "Frost's countryside is neither simple nor idyllic" is undercut by Cooper's insinuation that the narrator in "The Tuft of Flowers" finds safe haven and certainty through an uncomplicated, untroubled companionship within nature.

My essay argues that "The Tuft of Flowers" portrays nature as an inherently disruptive, unruly force, reversing the rural-urban dichotomy mentioned above. For Frost's narrator, human-constructed space demands a systematic, regimented, compliant mindset, whereas wild space engenders a transgressive form of uncertainty and chaos. Thus, the poem advances a *'wildered* mentality, consisting of two steps that motivate readers to confront the crises of modern life instead of retreating into an illusory bucolic ideal. First, the narrator's unquestioned adherence to the status quo is bewildered, which

123

undermines tightly held, socially constructed certainties. Second, his relationships with natural and human environments are wildered, which facilitates a transformation from estrangement to kinship. The ensuing partnerships spur ecological awareness and social improvement, but only if they accommodate doubt and disorder.

The setting of Frost's poem is rural New England, yet the fact that the narrator is inspired by a solitary stand of flowers resisting the domination humanity extends over the surrounding meadow indicates a wildered experience could occur in any constructed location, even a major metropolis. This mentality is now a basic tenet of the modern environmental movement. Eco-activists press the general public to choose a wildered mentality in both natural and constructed spaces, urging sustainable practices to curb resource extraction, habitat destruction, and waste. Large nonprofit organizations like the Wild Seed Project, the Nature Foundation, and Rewilding Britain, along with local community groups like Rewild Portland direct people to reject the socialized mandate of overconsumption and take steps to conserve threatened ecosystems, starting with their own homes and neighborhoods. These organizations rally concerned residents with provocative photographs and language, including a call to "rewild" human-inhabited places. Coined in 1990,[5] the term revitalizes the wildered principle of honoring nature's innate value and acting on behalf of ecologic processes, thereby spurning the false supremacy of human civilization.

Frost knew and enjoyed the natural world through active engagement as a hiker, an amateur botanist, and, for a time, a farmer.[6] Though not a staunch eco-critic, Frost "developed his poetic idiom"[7] living and working on his farm, an experience that, according to Thomas Bailey, prompted "a body of poetry marked by an acute environmental awareness,"[8] with works representing "Frost's prophetic, even profound environmental consciousness."[9] Frost's use of "wildered" is a throwback to an earlier age. Though the word was falling out of use[10] when Frost began writing "ecopoetry"[11] like "The Tuft of Flowers," it appeared frequently in eighteenth- and nineteenth-century poems that helped mold his poetic voice.[12] The wildered revelation was a common trope among Romantic poets, specifying an interdependent relationship between humans and nature based on a wildness they witnessed without and within. For these poets, a wildered experience goes beyond celebrating landscape; it transcends the material universe by exciting people's need to understand their humanity, build stronger communities, and forge a spiritual connection with nature.

Although Frost was born after the Romantic era, Amelia Klein attests, "Frost shares with his romantic forebears a vision of the natural world as the source and context of our lives."[13] The biosphere, for him, was more than a backdrop for human achievement or a set of exchangeable assets. Like the Romantics, Frost respected it as an activating force that provokes serious self-examination and disrupts the accepted social order. He did add the modern scientific perspective that the universe is unconcerned with human needs and problems, a perturbing uncertainty for many. Jonathan Barron contends that Frost addresses that particular uncertainty in "The Black Cottage" (1914), a response to Wordsworth's "The Ruined Cottage" (1797), by using nature to illuminate the "psychological need born of a newly awakened fear that in both the social and natural worlds one meets mostly with indifference."[14] People typically react to this indifference by seeking solace in the orderliness of social conventions and adopting a false certainty about humanity's importance and authority in the universe. However, Frost indicates that those who cling to a supposed right to commodify, dominate, and exploit the earth suffer crippling isolation, an impenetrable barrier that separates people from the natural world and each other.

Frost's "The Tuft of Flowers" is a response to existential angst, countering fears of cosmic indifference and life's meaninglessness. The poem challenges readers with a wildered event that echoes the Romantic epiphany, that is, Wordsworth's "spots of time,"[15] in which natural phenomena offer insight into the human condition and energize solidarity with place. Not a static refuge, nature's dynamism stirs thought and action. A butterfly and a clump of flowers bewilder the narrator's preconceived attitudes and assumptions about society and himself, freeing him from the certainty of a human exceptionalism that endorses arrogance, greed, and selfishness. Espousing uncertainty, the wildered narrator intimates that readers should surpass the simple demands of daily life and engage in the work of sustaining natural processes and reestablishing true human community.

CONSTRUCTED CERTAINTY

The poem, which consists of twenty-one rhymed couplets, begins by setting a constructed scene and introducing a dissatisfied narrator.

Speaking in first person, a hay-turner begins raking a meadow several hours after a mower has cut the grass.

> I went to turn the grass once after one
> Who mowed it in the dew before the sun.
>
> The dew was gone that made his blade so keen
> Before I came to view the levelled scene.
>
> I looked for him behind an isle of trees;
> I listened for his whetstone on the breeze.
>
> But he had gone his way, the grass all mown,
> And I must be, as he had been,—alone,
>
> 'As all must be,' I said within my heart,
> 'Whether they work together or apart.'[16]

The early couplets outline the narrator's sense of seclusion and loss. The location is disconcerting because the trees are an island unto themselves, the dew has dissipated, withered flowers lay cut on the ground, the breeze no longer carries the sound of a comrade, and grass lies dead in heaps everywhere. The mower's destructive flattening and orderly evening of the meadow gives the whole area an unnatural uniformity, a barrenness. The hay-turner bears witness to a wasteland as he takes in the entirety of the situation. He is disillusioned by the certainty of humanity's coordinated efforts to control the natural space and harvest all usable resources. As the poem soon shows, he initially dismisses the butterfly's pointless quest for flowers from "yesterday's delight," criticizing the insect's optimism as he experiences the hopelessness of "memories grown dim." The narrator feels lost and dejected, laid low by the certainty imposed by human civilization.

Although the narrator works in the same space as the mower, he feels as separated from his compatriot as from the land. The gulf or barrier separating them seems more sociopsychological than material since it exists "within [his] heart" and springs, as Cooper surmises, from "quintessential twentieth-century anxieties, the fear of anonymity and alienation."[17] Nevertheless, the power and permanence of these existential anxieties are certain to the narrator, evident by his repetition of "must": "I must be . . . alone, / 'As all must be.'" Like the neighbor in Frost's "Mending Wall" (1914) who mindlessly repeats the customary attitude, "Good fences make good neighbors,"[18] the hay-turner initially repeats the standard belief that individual consciousnesses cannot intertwine and kindred spirits cannot communicate, a modernist absolute that leaves people lonely, afraid, bereft.

As stated earlier, the poem's natural setting belies a constructed space. The "levelled scene" is human-dominated, a meadow managed and owned rather than wild and free. The mower and the hay-turner play the role of civilization's tool, human machines expected to follow directions without independent thought or complicating emotions. In a classic example of capitalistic division of labor, the two men are singled out and set apart to do specialized jobs that alienate them from their work, its product, other workers, and their own humanity. The hay-turner sees himself and the mower as soulless instruments of economic domination. He imagines, to his horror, that once a task is complete—that is, "the grass all mown"—the worker ceases to exist, disappearing like the dew. First, the solitary mower has "gone his way" into oblivion, followed by, presumably, the narrator himself.

Because he appears first, the mower has more opportunity to experience the space as an untouched landscape. The hay-turner arrives after the mower has leveled the meadow and "the sun" of certainty, radiating enlightened rationality, has melted away his sense of natural wonder and brotherhood. The narrator indicates that capitalistic society has tasked him and the mower with exploiting nature, the lion share of the profits presumedly going to someone who does not live or work locally. Exacerbating the problem, nature participates in its own demise, as the fresh morning dew sharpens the mower's blade and helps him ravage the grassy meadow, reducing it to a resource for extraction. Dispirited, the narrator conducts a half-hearted search for association with the mower and the land by looking among the trees and listening to the breeze. He concedes that the isolation and fragmentation accompanying humanity's acts of destruction are the inescapable fate of modern life. He needs a wildered event to break the certainty, which will cause him to recharacterize the mower from automaton, a mere tool of socioeconomic forces, to feeling confederate, an agent of chaos.

WILDERED

At a moment of heartbreaking loneliness, when the constructed certainty of modern society has eroded any hope or sense of meaning, the hay-turner has his wildered experience.

> But as I said it, swift there passed me by
> On noiseless wing a 'wildered butterfly,
>
> Seeking with memories grown dim o'er night
> Some resting flower of yesterday's delight.
>
> And once I marked his flight go round and round,
> As where some flower lay withering on the ground.
>
> And then he flew as far as eye could see,
> And then on tremulous wing came back to me.
>
> I thought of questions that have no reply,
> And would have turned to toss the grass to dry;
>
> But he turned first, and led my eye to look
> At a tall tuft of flowers beside a brook,
>
> A leaping tongue of bloom the scythe had spared
> Beside a reedy brook the scythe had bared.
>
> I left my place to know them by their name,
> Finding them butterfly weed when I came.[19]

Frost himself experienced mowing and raking grass firsthand during his ownership of a farm in Derry, New Hampshire. This experience, along with his lifelong interest in natural processes, led the poet to infuse "his pastoral [poems] with the truth of ecology."[20] A keen observer of nature, Frost marks the flight of a butterfly searching for pollen as swift, silent, and, most importantly, uncertain. His fascination with botany compels him to identify the flower preserved by the mower as "butterfly weed." Noting his accuracy with scientific detail and acknowledgment of the beauty of natural phenomenon, Glenn

Adelson and John Elder proclaim that "to find Frost's equal as a poetic naturalist, one would have to go back to Shakespeare and John Clare."[21] Clare's poem "Patty" (1820) conflates "wilder'd scenes"[22] with a love for nature, a sense of freedom, and a deep need for self-reflection. Frost's narrator in "The Tuft of Flowers" is wildered into self-reflection that drives ecological concern and social reconnection.

The elided 'wildered ties the narrator's revelation to a sense of wildering and a sense of bewildering. The butterfly's flight represents the uncertainty and chaos inherent in a wildered mentality. However, an inability to locate "the flower of yesterday's delight," presumably because yesterday's flower likely "lay withering on the ground," indicates that to have a wildered revelation one must bewilder common assumptions and expectations, rejecting entrenched social attitudes and abandoning traditional "memories grown dim o're night." According to Hubert Zapf, the butterfly "draws the speaker's attention to the lively sphere of the natural world, the drama in miniature of loss, crisis, suffering, search, and disorientation through which the butterfly must go because of the utilitarian human intervention in and cultivation of the nonhuman world."[23] Parvin Ghasemi and Elham Mansooji explain that the disorientation leads to an "examination of the confrontation between man and the natural world, which ultimately leads to man confronting himself."[24] This process will not be certain or straight; it can be only haphazard and unsettled, a wild immersion into "questions that have no reply."

Curiously, the articulation of the word "wildered" in "The Tuft of Flowers" changed during its publication history. When it appeared on the front page of the newspaper *Derry Enterprise* (1906) and in Frost's first book of poetry *A Boy's Will* (1913), the line reads, "On noiseless wing a 'wildered butterfly."[25] However, the line reads, "On noiseless wing a bewildered butterfly,"[26] in later publications Frost approved, including *Selected Poems* (1923) and *Complete Poems of Robert Frost* (1949). Of course, the apostrophe in early versions of the poem means that 'wildered should be understood as "bewildered." From a stylistic standpoint, the omission of "be-" maintains the poetic meter, just as the single syllable "o're" does in the following line. Without the extra syllable, the lines match the iambic pentameter of the rest of the poem. Perhaps one reason Frost added the prefix in later versions was to give the line a more offbeat, bewildered rhythm, an uncertain meter to emphasize the seemingly random, disorganized flight of the butterfly and match the theme of confusion about people's relationship with nature and each other. The original version, though, directs readers to consider a wildered resolution.

Tracing the word's origin, the *Oxford English Dictionary* (*OED*) postulates that wildered[27] comes from the Middle Dutch *verwilderen* or German *verwildern*. The Dutch *verwilderen* translates as, "run wild; to go out of control."[28] The German *verwildern* translates as, "to become overgrown; to become feral."[29] The word has been used since the seventeenth century to identify negative[30] and positive[31] utilization of humanity's brute instincts. It represents a wildness that defies the confining habits of civilization and puts people in touch with their own untamed will. They must become feral to break free of society's norms and actively run wild or go out of control to explore possibilities beyond civilization's boundaries.

In English, wildered predates bewildered, the prefix "be-" added later to form an intensive verb that makes bewildered the quality of being thoroughly or excessively wildered. Comparing entries in the *OED*, "wildered" and "bewildered" have the overlapping definitions of losing one's way or path and being mentally perplexed, befuddled. However, wildered has one additional definition that bewildered does not: "(of a place or region) in which one may lose one's way; pathless, wild."[32] Both words indicate a confused state of mind, but wildered locates that confusion in an unrestrained geographic space. Therefore, a wildered mind or spirit resists becoming "tamed and cultivated";[33] it disorders conventional assumptions in a quest for an authentic life. This quality of wildness can be found in the natural world and one's own primal nature. Not just a confused or bewildered state of mind, wildered is the arousal of intense feelings and a deeper awareness of one's selfhood, including one's place in the natural environment. This facet may be a reason the word resonated so strongly with Romantic poets Percy Bysshe Shelley, John Keats, and Samuel Coleridge, in addition to Alexander Pope, Charlotte Brontë, Walter Scott, William Blake, Rudyard Kipling, and a host of lesser-known poets.

Returning to Frost's "The Tuft of Flowers," bewildered is an appropriate adjective since the flight of a butterfly, unsure and pathless, matches the uncertainty of the hay-turner who begins the poem feeling physically isolated and spiritually lonely. Rather than remain in this confused state, however, he transforms after his eye and his imagination are drawn to a wildered place by the butterfly. His hopelessness is challenged by a patch of flowers, spared from destruction. The uncultivated space rouses uncertainty about human supremacy and induces a joyfulness about life, beauty, and wildness, the first step in rewilding his attitude toward the local ecosystem.

This route to existential and ecological enlightenment demands the hay-turner first submit to the chaos of bewilderment, something most people resist. Then, he must initiate a wildered mindset to navigate successfully through that confusion, as through a storm, instead of retreating into the calm port of certainty. Sheldon Liebman states that for Frost, "revelation is not just an escape from confusion and disappointment but a consequence of them."[34] Thus, the truth seeker should not avoid what Frost, in a 1935 "Letter" to the *Amherst Student*, refers to as the "black and utter chaos"[35] of human existence. One must become (be)wildered by voluntarily walking beyond the outskirts of social expectations in the rain at midnight, as in Frost's poem "Acquainted with the Night" (1928), or hiking up a rough mountainside to enter the dark woods of intellectual doubt, as in "Two Look at Two" (1923). In a 1927 letter to Leonidas Payne Jr., Frost explicates his intention, "My poems—I should suppose everybody's poems—are all set to trip the reader head and foremost into the boundless. Ever since infancy I have had the habit of leaving my blocks carts chairs and such like ordinaries where people would be pretty sure to fall forward over them in the dark. Forward, you understand, *and* in the dark."[36] Therefore, stepping into the wildered darkness creates a temporary bewildered state that leads one forward into honest, intense assessment of the human-nature relationship. In Frost's "The Tuft of Flowers," it leads strangers to form an unspoken pact to act as rewilding agents. They share a burgeoning need to "restore an area of land or whole landscape to its natural uncultivated state."[37]

KINDRED SPIRITS

Frost believed that nature resists containment and domination, evident by the disruptive "something" in "Mending Wall." He proposed that this dynamic force is irrevocably linked to humanity's material survival and social cohesion. According to Virginia Smith, his poems "remind us that humans are *a part* of nature and cannot be *apart* from it."[38] The implication is that people have a responsibility to themselves to protect the biosphere, which demands "a genuine exchange, a reciprocity."[39] Ecological reciprocity is a radical act, requiring humility before nature's authority and courage to reconnect with the wildness in one's personal nature. This genuine exchange, to Frost, is also essential for a healthy society. Klein indicates that "Mending Wall" advises people to adopt what I am calling a wildered mentality and join the natural "forces of disorder"[40] that disturb the barriers of human certainty because "community, Frost intimates, can only be sustained through such disruptions."

A similar message about disruption and sustainability appears at the end of "The Tuft of Flowers."

> The mower in the dew had loved them thus,
> By leaving them to flourish, not for us,
>
> Nor yet to draw one thought of ours to him.
> But from sheer morning gladness at the brim.
>
> The butterfly and I had lit upon,
> Nevertheless, a message from the dawn,
>
> That made me hear the wakening birds around,
> And hear his long scythe whispering to the ground,
>
> And feel a spirit kindred to my own;
> So that henceforth I worked no more alone;
>
> But glad with him, I worked as with his aid,
> And weary, sought at noon with him the shade;
>
> And dreaming, as it were, held brotherly speech
> With one whose thought I had not hoped to reach.
>
> 'Men work together,' I told him from the heart,
> 'Whether they work together or apart.' (25–40)[41]

Here, the narrator's wildered experience disrupts his work clearing the meadow and disorders his sense of alienation from nature and fellow humans. Feeling "a spirit kindred to my own" seems to refer more to the mower than the butterfly, but the social connection relies on an ecological one. Because the hay-turner's revelatory moment occurs at a specific time and place, he and the insect commune in a way that the two men do not. It is the man with the butterfly, not the mower, who "had lit upon . . . a message from the dawn." The verb "lit" evokes three different meanings in this case: to discover by chance, to settle or land on, and to illuminate or ignite. The hay-turner's experience is unexpected, concrete, and enlightening; plus, it is unrelated to the mower's own experience of wildered revelation. These revelations are the basis for their dream of "brotherly speech," which heightens their awareness about the value of the natural world. This appreciation is tempered by the economic need to harvest the grass, shown in a couplet that aligns the sound of "wakening birds" and the sound of the mower's "long scythe." However, conflict between wild nature and violent human civilization need not succumb to a zero-sum-game resolution. Instead, Frost's narrator dreams of a negotiation that serves all parties.

Recognizing nature as uncertain and "in flux,"[42] Frost created a poetic persona who carefully inspects his surroundings and himself, modeling a mental and emotional flexibility that allows him to reevaluate his cosmic role and cross "the line where man leaves off and nature starts." This liminal position bewilders him at first because it represents a divergence from the traditional associations people have with nature, namely their desire to achieve domination over it or transcendence beyond it. Nevertheless, Frost's narrator finds his footing and grasps his role in nature's cycles, the first step to acquiring a wildered self. Frost explains in his 1939 essay "The Figure a Poem Makes" that he inserted "wildness pure"[43] into the content and style of his poetry not only to delight the reader but also to ignite serious self-reflection. His goal was a "wildness of logic"[44] that occurs only after one adopts a wildered sensibility, causing a revelation that "must be more felt than seen ahead like prophecy." In Frost's poems, attaining the deeper meaning of human existence in an indifferent universe requires renouncing custom, embracing uncertainty, and throwing oneself into wild(er)ness.

In "The Tuft of Flowers," the wildered experience also opens one to valuing nature for its own sake. A crucial component of the narrator's revelation is that the mower does not preserve the flowers for the benefit of the hay-turner or the butterfly, or to establish a connection between himself and the hay-turner. The mower's motivation comes "from sheer morning gladness," a spontaneous and illogical response that cannot be denied or contained. His act, or really the staying of an act he is supposed to perform, is powerful and pure, a wildered moment of emotion "at the brim" that is individual and intuitive without the intrusion of social expectation. Not mowing a portion of the meadow makes him less productive, but he earns "the added value of not using a resource,"[45] an important lesson since "no bottom line can adequately express the value of the sanity, health, pleasure, and rest that can be gleaned from nature, nor the value of working and living in a community with shared values and goals." Echoing the butterfly metaphor, the man's fundamental nature has undergone a metamorphosis.

Seeing the flowers spared by the mower creates a heightened emotional reaction in the hay-turner, causing him to imagine the absent mower by his side. However, the mower is not physically there, so the hay-turner must unearth and nurture his own feelings about humanity's role in the natural and social realms. The mower and the hay-turner each initiate a personal dialogue with nature, a "brotherly speech" conveyed "from the heart" and born out of sincere "gladness." It speaks of their obligation to consider nature's interests, as well as humanity's own spiritual health, rather than surrender completely to arrogant self-interest or a hopeless sense of despair and abandonment.

Frost's essay "The Figure a Poem Makes" indicates that poetry's purpose is to unsettle and challenge readers. "The Tuft of Flowers" harnesses bewilderment to resist the status quo and confound restraint so wisdom can sing. The wildered poem supplies readers a path through chaos and uncertainty, not around them; it uses the reader's imagination, a type of mental wildness, to secure valuable insights. As Frost's essay declares, "If it is a wild tune, it is a Poem."[46] This mentality appears in Frost's poem "Wild Grapes" (1923) as the speaker, a young girl, experiences a wildered moment of becoming the fruit hanging from a white birch's upper limbs. She forgoes attempting to control the tree, which means, "The opposite was true. The tree had [her]."[47] Also, "For Once, Then, Something" (1923) features a wildered moment of clarity, contrasting humanity's superficial, self-absorbed approach to life. At first, the narrator only sees his "godlike"[48] self when looking into a well, but then he has a revelation: "I discerned, as I thought, beyond the picture, / Through the picture, a something white, uncertain, / Something more of the depths." Once the man's self-satisfaction and certainty become uncertain and bewildered, he is open to a wildered sensibility that allows him to penetrate the confusion of existence and emerge into a state of understanding.

These hard-earned lessons mirror Frost's own life experiences, the perspicacity gained from his (be)wildered spirit: "All I would keep for myself is the freedom of the material—the condition of body and mind now and then to summon aptly from the vast chaos of all I have lived through."[49] By facing the chaos, Frost shares with his readers the inspiration to persevere, to (be)wilder societal restraint and attain ecological cognizance. Klein asserts that Frost's poems "dare us to be radical, to overturn all and start from scratch—to 'pass through' to whatever may be on the other side of the established social order."[50] In "The Tuft of Flowers," the hay-turner models a (be)wildered reverie, an imagined excursion into the wild where the individual contemplates his circumstances and changes his perspective. The hay-turner, like a butterfly, transforms. He turns from bewildered nihilist to wildered humanist through the guidance of nature, as Fred Schroeder confirms, "when Robert Frost wants to tell us that 'Men work together whether they work together or apart'—certainly a bodiless abstraction—he exemplifies the abstraction by attaching it to two natural symbols, a tuft of flowers and a butterfly, which he has detached from the confusion of nature in general."[51] It is the concrete and familiar that helps readers penetrate the uncertainties of the natural world and human nature.

It should be emphasized that Frost was not idealistic about nature; in fact, Eric Link admits many of his poems show "skepticism concerning the ability of the poet to reconcile man and Nature."[52] Although the hay-turner hears "the wakening birds around" and the "leaping tongue" of the flowers, his naming the plant in the human tongue is an act of control over nature's agency. It seems his intent is not to dominate but to quit the entrenched human mindset and learn. In the line "I left my place to know them by their name," he voluntarily relinquishes human superiority to know, befriend, appreciate a plant's individual identity. Clearly, the natural space profoundly affects the hay-turner, who stops raking the grass and commits to paying careful attention to the butterfly's wildered flight. At first, it circles unpredictably and extends to the edge of his sight, pushing him to see beyond the immediate and superficial. When it returns, the man allows the butterfly to guide him, so together they "lit upon" the signifier, a brilliantly blooming tuft of flowers, and the signified, "a message from the dawn." It is a message of kinship with nature's cycles and fellow humans.

The poem presents a (be)wildered journey that takes the narrator from isolation to community, a healthy environment populated by like-minded people, symbolized by the mower, instead of a wasteland of one. Frost found his own sense of community through public readings of "The Tuft of Flowers," an experience he described "as both the agent and the emblem of his return to other people."[53] For poets and readers, the separation of space or time does not eliminate the ability to sing a wild tune together. The hay-turner realizes this after his wildered imagination reframes his notion of loneliness. The mower may be absent, but his actions suggest a mentality upon which the hay-turner finds common ground. He and the mower take independent paths to the flowers and the sensibility they represent, "sheer morning gladness at the brim." Hence, embracing chaos and confusion leads to a genuine passion for place and people, a true alliance to a dynamic, unmasterable, and wildered world that Frost considered "the source and context of our lives."[54] Community, whether social or ecological, relies on interdependent relationships.

The relationship between "The Tuft of Flowers" and "Mending Wall" further illuminates how Frost positioned nature as an important dynamic force and a means to address human isolation. In *North of Boston*, the page preceding the poem states, "*Mending Wall* takes up the theme where *A Tuft of Flowers* in *A Boy's Will* laid it down."[55] The speaker in "Mending Wall" balks when his neighbor thoughtlessly repeats the unneighborly maxim, "Good fences make good neighbors." He questions the attitude of physical division and emotional detachment, concerned about "What I was walling in or walling out." An unknown but very real "something" in the natural world and in human nature resists this type of separation. According to Klein, the poem intimates that a "vital connection between nature and poetry, the involvement of man-made meanings in the bodily workings of the world, is what permits us not to escape from but to 'go behind' our father's sayings and the empty echoes of a false hegemony."[56] A similar connection to nature empowers the hay-turner in "The Tuft of Flowers" to confront and go behind the chaos and uncertainty to gain understanding and renewal. The "something" in this poem is a butterfly and a clump of flowers, which turns the narrator's outlook from inward despair to outward wonder and regard for the earth. It is clear, as Zapf affirms, that "the renewed relationship of culture to nature becomes an inspiration for the renewal of the relationship of human beings to each other."[57] It is a social connection born of two wildered experiences.

The final couplet implies the hay-turner and the mower establish a spiritual connection that carries ecological responsibilities. Most scholars analyze the connection itself, focusing on the word "together."

Cooper insists the poem rejects the "isolation, extinction, and that nervous apprehension among the moderns of disappointment at how actual human beings have failed to live up to the humanist ideals"[58] because "the speaker finds he can hold 'brotherly speech' with the mower and make of that discourse a new imagined community." Jonathan Levin posits that their collaboration turns labor into play, which "transforms the atmosphere of the poem from resigned isolation to exuberant connectivity."[59] Dana Cairns Watson examines this connection through an economic lens, arguing for the value of humans "working together, with pleasure if less efficiently."[60] However, I believe the important word in these lines is "work"—the tasks and duties all members of Cooper's imagined community should accomplish once they learn to cooperate. They take on the work of developing one's best self, the work of finding common ground with strangers, and the work of protecting and preserving the natural environment.

The hay-turner is receptive to nature's message because he is a local, an insider who lives and works on previously uncultivated natural spaces. He is developing an "environmental consciousness"[61] that Ethan Mannon spots in Frost's poetry. It is a radical form of "georgic environmentalism,"[62] which is important to eco-critics as it "speaks directly to resource conservation and sustainability." The hay-turner's rootedness in a rural place does not mean he has escaped human civilization; the work he and the mower do in the meadow shows they bring an oppressive civilizing influence with them. Rootedness means he can perceive and enter the chaos of a natural system. It may also mean being closer to wanting to do the work of balancing ecological and economic needs. Moreover, Mannon argues that georgic texts by Frost and other poets remind "us that if Yellowstone and Central Park are sacred, so, too, are agricultural lands and forests, suburbs and city blocks."[63] Led by this sentiment, the twenty-first-century rewilding movement encourages urban dwellers and suburbanites to find a sense of rootedness and initiate environmental activism as insiders of cultivated natural spaces.

(Re)wildered in the Twenty-First Century

Frost's poetry endorses a wildered approach to life, tying the value of deep intellectual and emotional self-investigation to wild places and a mindset of uncertainty. For example, he asserts in "New Hampshire" (1923), "The more the sensibilitist I am / The more I seem to want my mountains wild."[64] His "The Line-Gang" (1916) criticizes the invasion of modern life, alerting readers that telephone and telegraph lines "throw a forest down less cut than broken" and "set the wild at naught."[65] In addition, "The Last Mowing" (1928) celebrates wildflowers that thrive when farmers stop mowing and plowing a meadow, though the narrator worries trees may crowd out the flowers because "the meadow is done with the tame."[66] The desired outcome seems to be a better understanding of human existence, from the wisdom of one's primary instincts to a collective responsibility for the health of the natural world.

Even if few today use the term "wildered," the attitude it represents drives a powerful strain of environmentalism. Twenty-first-century cultural ecology, or a study of "the interaction and living interrelationship between culture and nature,"[67] decenters human dominion and forwards a rewildered mindset. "Rewilderness is the return to nature's own will, not a human imposition of a 'right' ecosystem or assemblage abstaining from governing nature."[68] To save local ecosystems, some environmentalists urge humans to rewild their thinking and daily choices, based on "embodied and situated experiencing."[69]

Anticipating the rewildered movement, Frost's hay-turner in "The Tuft of Flowers" undergoes an embodied and situated experience that makes him acutely aware of his location's particularity and his own physicality. Experiencing the landscape disrupts his internal musing, activating his senses and elevating the biotic to the point that the birds and flowers have voice. The hay-turner further acknowledges his being in a specific natural place by identifying by name of the plant that has resisted the reaper's blade as butterfly weed (*Asclepias tuberosa*) while he and the mower remain nameless. As stated above, naming a plant gives humans some control over it, yet differentiating it from other species of flowers gives it identity, a selfhood to be respected as opposed to an asset to be exploited. Place has authority over the man, suggested by his inability to ignore the butterfly, which turns his attention away from the work of resource extraction. The choice by each man to allow the tuft of flowers to flourish, when their jobs are to destroy and harvest, is a rewildered act. As with other rewildered landscapes, the small island of butterfly weed surrounded by a sea of cut grass represents a pocket of "fertility and growth, but not one of economy and expansion. Rewildered landscapes are ruins of a civilizational ethos."[70] Frost's wildered attitude confounds that ethos, as the butterfly spins the hay-turner around and around to unsettle the legitimacy of human domination and destruction. Seeing the flowers alerts him that he is not alone, either as a member of human society or as a member of the biosphere. As Pujita Guha avers, "It is in a rewildered space that life sees resurgence of energy." Pushed to cooperate with nature, the hay-turner gains a new perspective that rejuvenates him.

This resurgence has impelled the environmental movement to revive the word "wildered" and rebrand it. The Wild Seed Project conveys on its website, "The term rewilding first appeared in the conservation world in the 1980s with a continental-scale vision to protect large tracts of wilderness and connect these areas with migration corridors."[71] The current rewilder movement ambitiously seeks to do more than preserve existing wilderness. Rewilding[72] is a process of ecological and cultural rejuvenation, which, according to Rewild.com, includes "restoring ancestral ways of living that create greater health and well-being for humans and the ecosystems that we belong to."[73] However, returning an ecosystem to its natural state and changing the ways people live in a modern consumer culture takes time, money, and resolve. It requires an approach that is sustainable ecologically and economically.

A rewildered approach is all-encompassing, requiring humans to "come together in a desire to rewild our homes, our communities, and ourselves."[74] The reasons to rewild are diverse, though largely human-centered, including "concern over ecological collapse or economic uncertainty, health problems, a nagging sense of something missing in life, or a desire to 'save the world.'" Perhaps this effort needs to be self-serving, at least initially, since prevailing ideologies privilege human needs and interests. Advocates of rewilding want people to come to their senses, figuratively and literally, so they recognize nature as part of their community and them a part of its. A rewildered community can occur only if its members, such as Frost's hay-turner and mower, learn "how to cooperate, how to make decisions as a community, and how to repair strained relationships." Once people commit to cooperation, they may be able to accept the compromise and sacrifice it demands. The True Nature Foundation explains that place is not rewildered unless it is "a self-regulatory and self-sustaining stable ecosystem, possibly with near pre-human levels of biodiversity." Therefore, an untouched tuft of flowers imparts the first glimmer of a rewildered ethos.

Achieving pre-human levels of biodiversity is a challenge in remote locations, so it seems impossible to rewild more populated areas. Nevertheless, environmental education and activism is currently at work on a citywide scale through nonprofit organizations like Rewild Portland. Since 2009, the Oregon organization has prioritized incorporating environmental preservation with social justice "to learn how to integrate our culture into the landscape in a way that is regenerative rather than extractive."[75] Just as Frost indicated, ecological regeneration must be a collaborative, grassroots undertaking. Across the nation in Portland, Maine, the Wild Seed Project seeks to "rekindle the sense of wildness and connection to the natural world that we crave."[76] Their website describes projects people can do at their homes and in their communities: planting native shrubs, adopting a street tree or "sidewalk hellstrip" to care for, transforming a lawn into meadow by not mowing. Rewilding Britain calls this approach "urban rewilding."[77] It is part of a concerted effort to rewild individual neighborhoods and make them "a safe haven for butterflies and birds,"[78] and perhaps tufts of flowers. These organizations argue for environmentalism as a moral necessity that has the added benefit of recreating a sense of community in the modern world. This ideology upholds Frost's final statement about humans cooperating for a common good, "'Whether they work together or apart.'"

The success of the rewilder movement depends on people's relationships with the natural world, each other, and themselves. Throughout his life, Frost worked the land, noting that among his vocations farming did the most to mold his writing.[79] It helped him shake off conventional thinking and boldly confront the limits of modern life. His speaker in "New Hampshire" initially ponders whether he should run from nature in fear or find excuses not to act in nature's best interest. In the end, he rejects both, proudly declaring, "I choose to be a plain New Hampshire farmer."[80] Written from the position of rooted insider, Frost's nature poems are (re)wildered, testifying to the humility and hard work needed to imagine and enact a sustainable future.

WORKS CITED

Adelson, Glenn, and John Elder. "Robert Frost's Ecosystem of Meanings in 'Spring Pools.'" *Interdisciplinary Studies in Literature and Environment* 13, no. 2 (2006): 1–17.

Bailey, Thomas. "Reading Robert Frost Environmentally: Contexts Then and Now." In *Robert Frost in Context*, edited by Mark Richardson, 241–49. Cambridge: Cambridge University Press, 2014.

Barron, Jonathan N. "A Tale of Two Cottages: Frost and Wordsworth." In *Roads Not Taken: Rereading Robert Frost*, edited by Earl J. Wilcox and Jonathan N. Barron, 132–52. Columbia: University of Missouri Press, 2000.

"Bewildered." *Oxford English Dictionary, Vol. I*. Oxford: Oxford University Press, 1961.

Bronte, Charlotte. *Villette*. New York: J. M. Dent & Sons, 1922.

Carver, Steve. "Rewilding . . . Conservation and Conflict." *ECOS* 37, no. 2 (2016): 2–10.

Chapman, H. Perry. "Persona and Myth in Houbraken's Life of Jan Steen." *The Art Bulletin* 75, no. 1 (1993): 135–50.

Clare, John. *Poems Descriptive of Rural Life and Scenery*. London: Taylor and Hessey, 1820.

Coleridge, Samuel Taylor. *Christabel*. London: Henry Frowde, 1907.

Cooper, John Xiros. "Robert Frost and Modernism." In *Robert Frost in Context*, edited by Mark Richardson, 85–91. Cambridge: Cambridge University Press, 2014.

Diaconu, Madalina. "Matter, Movement, Memory Footnotes to an Urban Tactile Design." In *Senses and the City: An Interdisciplinary Approach to Urban Sensescapes*, edited by Madalina Diaconu, Eva Heuberger, Ruth Mateus-Berr, and Lukas Marcel Vosicky, 13–32. Piscataway: Transaction, 2001.

Dickey, Frances. "Frost's 'The Tuft of Flowers': A Problem of Other Minds." *The New England Quarterly* 75, no. 2 (2002): 299–311.

Eigler, Friederike. "Engendering German Nationalism: Gender and Race in Frieda von Bülow's Colonial Writings." In *The Imperialistic Imagination: German Colonialism and Its Legacy*, edited by Sara Friedrichsmeyer, Sara Lennox, and Susanne Zantop, 69–88. Ann Arbor: University of Michigan Press, 1998.

Eisenberg, Ram. "Rewilding Thinking." *International Interdisciplinary Symposium, Surviving the Anthropocene: Towards Elemental Literacy and Interdisciplinary Partnerships, Programme and Abstracts*. May 24–26, 2021.

Faggen, Robert. "Frost and the Questions of Pastoral." In *The Cambridge Companion to Robert Frost*, edited by Robert Faggen, 49–74. Cambridge: Cambridge University Press, 2001.

Francis, Lesley Lee. "The Derry Years of Robert Frost." In *Robert Frost in Context*, edited by Mark Richardson, 263–70. Cambridge: Cambridge University Press, 2014.

Frost, Robert. *A Boy's Will*. New York: Henry Holt, 1915.

———. *The Collected Prose of Robert Frost*. Edited by Mark Richardson. Cambridge, MA: Harvard University Press, 2007.

———. *Mountain Interval*. New York: Henry Holt, 1931.

———. *New Hampshire*. New York: Henry Holt, 1923.

———. *North of Boston*. New York: Henry Holt, 1914.

———. *The Notebooks of Robert Frost*. Edited by Robert Faggen. Cambridge, MA: Harvard University Press, 2006.

———. *Robert Frost: Collected Poems, Prose, & Plays*. Edited by Richard Poirier and Mark Richardson. New York: The Library of America, 1995.

———. *Selected Poems*. New York: Henry Holt, 1923.

Ghasemi, Parvin, and Elham Mansooji. "Nature and Man in Robert Frost." *CLA Journal* 49, no. 4 (2006): 462–81.

Goddard, Julia. "The Deserted Garden." *Chambers's Journal of Popular Literature, Science, and Art* 718 (1877): 624.

Guha, Pujita. "A Century of Dying: Anthropocenic Imaginaries and the Cinema of Lav Diaz." MPhil thesis, Jawaharlal Nehru University, 2017.

Hass, Robert Bernard. "'Measuring Myself against all Creation': Robert Frost and Pastoral." In *Robert Frost in Context*, edited by Mark Richardson, 114–22. Cambridge: Cambridge University Press, 2014.

Hoffmann, John. "Kant's Aesthetic Categories: Race in the 'Critique of Judgment.'" *Aesthetic Speculations* 44, no. 2 (2016): 54–81.

Hogg, James. "A Night Piece." *The Poetical Register* 8 (1814): 90.

———. "Verses to the Comet of 1811." *Chamgers's Edinburgh Journal* 195 (1835): 312.

Jorgensen, Dolly. "Rethinking Rewilding." *Geoforum* 65 (2015): 482–88.

King, Henry. "To a Father on the Death of His Daughter." *The Mirror of Literature* 49 no. 11 (1847): 352.

Kipling, Rudyard. "In the Matter of One Compass." *The Collected Poems of Rudyard Kipling*. Hertfordshire: Wordsworth Poetry Library, 1994.

Klein, Amelia. "The Counterlove of Robert Frost." *Twentieth-Century Literature* 54, no. 3 (2008): 362–87.

Levin, Jonathan. "Robert Frost and Pragmatism." In *Robert Frost in Context*, edited by Mark Richardson, 135–41. Cambridge: Cambridge University Press, 2014.

Liebman, Sheldon W. "Robert Frost, Romantic." *Twentieth-Century Literature* 42, no. 4 (1996): 417–37.

Link, Eric Carl. "Nature's Extra-Vagrants: Frost and Thoreau in the Maine Woods." *Papers on Language and Literature* 33, no. 2 (1997): 182–97.

Mannon, Ethan. "Georgic Environmentalism in North of Boston." *Interdisciplinary Studies in Literature and Environment* 23, no. 2 (2016): 344–68.

Morris, William. *The Earthly Paradise: A Poem*. London: Longmans, Green, and Co., 1903.

"Nate Bjorge." *Sofar Sounds*. Accessed August 11, 2022. https://www.sofarsounds.com/artists/nate-bjorge.

Nolan, Sean. "'The Task that Leads the Wilder'd Mind': Robert Bloomfield, Humble Industry, and Studious Leisure." *European Romantic Review* 31, no. 5 (2020): 573–85.

"Our Core Values." *Rewild Portland*. Accessed June 7, 2022. https://www.rewildportland.com.

Patmore, Coventry. "Frederick Graham to His Mother." *Faithful for Ever*. Boson: Ticknor and Fields, 1861.

"Returning Native Plants to the Maine Landscape." *Wild Seed Project*. Accessed June 7, 2022. https://www.wildseedproject.net/2022/01/what-is-rewilding.

"Rewild." *Cambridge Dictionary*. Cambridge: Cambridge University Press. Accessed June 7, 2022. https://www.dictionary.cambridge.org/us/dictionary/english/rewild.

"Rewilding." *Rewild.com*. Accessed June 7, 2022. https://www.rewild.com.

"Rewilding Glossary." *Rewilding Britain*. Accessed July 31, 2023. https://www.rewildingbritain.org.uk/why-rewild/what-is-rewilding/rewilding-glossary.

Richardson, Mark. "Robert Frost." In *The Cambridge Companion to American Poets*. 160-71. Cambridge: Cambridge University Press, 2015.

Schroeder, Fred E. H. "Andrew Wyeth and the Transcendental Tradition." *American Quarterly* 17, no. 3 (1965): 559–67.

Scott, Walter. *Scott's Rokeby: A Poem in Six Cantos*. New York: Macmillan, 1890.

Shelley, Percy Bysshe. *Queen Mab, with notes*. London: John Ascham, 1834.

———. "Song, Despair." *Original Poetry*. Poetry, edited by Richard Garnett. London: John Lane, 1898.

Smith, Virginia F. "Frost on the Apple." *Interdisciplinary Studies in Literature and Environment* 23, no. 4 (2016): 677–93.

Stoler, Ann L. "Sexual Affronts and Racial Frontiers: European Identities and the Cultural Politics of Exclusion in Colonial Southeast Asia." In *Theories of Race and Racism: A Reader*. Reader, edited by Les Back and John Solomos. 322-51. New York: Routledge, 2000.

Trevelyan, Robert Calverley. "Epimetheus." *Mallow and Asphodel*. New York: Macmillan, 1898."What Is Rewilding?"

True Nature Foundation. Accessed June 7, 2022. https://www.truenaturefoundation. org/what-is-rewilding.

"Verwilderen." *Cambridge Dictionary*. Cambridge: Cambridge University Press. Accessed June 7, 2022. https://www.dictionary.cambridge.org/dictionary/ dutch-english/verwilderen.

"Verwildern." *Cambridge Dictionary*. Cambridge: Cambridge University Press. Accessed June 7, 2022. https://www.dictionary.cambridge.org/dictionary/ german-english/verwildern.

Wahrman, Dror. *Mr. Collier's Letter Racks: A Tale of Art and Illusion at the Threshold of the Modern Information Age*. Oxford: Oxford University Press, 2012.

Watson, Dana Cairns. "'New Terms of Worth." *Interdisciplinary Studies in Literature and Environment* 23, no. 2 (2016): 309–43.

"Wildered." *Oxford English Dictionary, Vol. XII*. Oxford: Oxford University Press, 1961.

Wordsworth, William. "The Prelude." *Wordsworth's Poetry and Prose*, edited by Nicholas Halmi. New York: W. W. Norton, 2014.

Zapf, Hubert. *Literature as Cultural Ecology: Sustainable Texts*. New York: Bloomsbury Academic, 2016.

———. "Robert Frost: An Ecological Perspective." *The Robert Frost Review* 14 (2004): 69–85.

ENDNOTES

1. Hass, "'Measuring Myself against all Creation,'" 115.
2. Hass, 116.
3. Faggen, "Frost and the Questions of Pastoral," 50.
4. Cooper, "Robert Frost and Modernism," 88.
5. Jorgensen, "Rethinking Rewilding," 482.
6. Smith, "Frost on the Apple," 678.
7. Francis, "The Derry Years of Robert Frost," 266.
8. Bailey, "Reading Robert Frost Environmentally," 241.
9. Bailey, 247.
10. The use of "wildered" has not totally disappeared from contemporary use. It is the current name of a folk band and appears in other groups' lyrics, such as pop singer Lisa Miskovsky's "Midnight Sun" (2003), heavy metal Defleshed's "Reclaim the Beat" (2005), and country singer Leah Blevins's "Mountain" (2021). Fantasy author Kate Elliott published *Throne of Eldraine: The Wildered Quest* (2019). In these examples, a wildered state occurs when one loses oneself to natural and/or psychological wildness. It represents a type of self-examination, a test of one's moral character that some pass and others fail.
11. Watson, "'New Terms of Worth,'" 312.
12. The Romantics, in particular, wrote of "wildered" thinking and experiences to identify a connection between wild spaces and the poetic imagination that disorders social norms and regenerates the human spirit. A wildered mentality serves the poet's desire to either elevate readers above the corruptive influence of industrialization, as in Percy Shelley's philosophical tract *Queen Mab* (1813), or reveal the horrors lurking in the human subconscious, as in Samuel Coleridge's Gothic romance "Christabel" (1816) and his conversation poem "The Eolian Harp" (1796). In these poems, intelligent and creative people access a wild part of their nature to see through the mental confusion of existence, gaining insight that is hidden from people who rely entirely on observation and reason. Wildered also expresses emotions triggered by trauma, such as war in Walter Scott's "Rokeby" (1813), grief in Shelley's "Song, Despair" (1810) and Julia Goddard's "The Deserted Garden" (1877), or death in Henry King's "To a Father on the Death of His Daughter" (1847) and William Morris's "The Earthly Paradise" (1903). On the other extreme, Charlotte Brontë's protagonist in *Villette* (1853) feels wildered after enjoying a wonderful day with someone she loves. For nineteenth-century pastoral poets, the word denotes a person's ecstatic recognition of the natural landscape's purity and beauty, as in James Hogg's "Verses to the Comet of 1811" and "A Night Piece" (1811) or Coventry Patmore's "Frederick Graham to His Mother" (1861). The word also indicates nature's dangerous power, as in Rudyard Kipling's "In the Matter of One Compass" (1892) or Robert Trevelyan's "Epimetheus" (1898).
13. Klein, "The Counterlove of Robert Frost," 362.
14. Barron, "A Tale of Two Cottages," 134.
15. Wordsworth, "The Prelude," 353.
16. Frost, *A Boy's Will*, 47.
17. Cooper, "Robert Frost and Modernism," 89.
18. Frost, *North of Boston*, 12.
19. Frost, *A Boy's Will*, 47-48.
20. Mannon, "Georgic Environmentalism in North of Boston," 346.
21. Adelson and Elder, "Robert Frost's Ecosystem of Meanings in 'Spring Pools,'" 2.
22. Clare, *Poems Descriptive of Rural Life and Scenery*, 152.

23. Zapf, "Robert Frost," 74.
24. Ghasemi and Mansooji, "Nature and Man in Robert Frost," 463.
25. Frost, A Boy's Will, 47.
26. Frost, Selected Poems, 64.
27. "Wildered," Oxford English Dictionary, 124.
28. "Verwilderen," Oxford English Dictionary.
29. "Verwildern," Oxford English Dictionary.
30. Dror Wahrman asserts in Mr. Collier's Letter Racks that seventeenth-century Dutch poet Joost van den Vondel used verwilderen to describe people who he considered uncivilized, debased. Ann Stoler in "Sexual Affronts and Racial Frontiers" connects the word to nineteenth-century racist assumptions held by Dutch colonists. John Hoffmann writes in "Kant's Aesthetic Categories" that philosopher Immanuel Kant included verwildern in a 1785 paper on racial essentialism, stating that the imagination, if not properly restrained, will cause humanity's degeneration or brutification. Friederike Eigler explains in "Engendering German Nationalism" that nineteenth-century German author Frieda von Bülow used it as a racist slur in a colonial novel about German East Africa.
31. H. Perry Chapman in "Persona and Myth in Houbraken's Life of Jan Steen" states that eighteenth-century Dutch painter Arnold Houbraken imbued verwilderen with a positive connotation, poetically praising fellow painter Jan Steen for his creatively undisciplined approach to art. Madalina Diaconu uses verwildern in "Matter, Movement, Memory Footnotes to an Urban Tactile Design" to praise ecologically minded architects.
32. "Wildered," Oxford English Dictionary, 124.
33. Nolan, "'The Task that Leads the Wilder'd Mind,'" 576.
34. Liebman, "Robert Frost, Romantic," 432.
35. Richardson, "Robert Frost," 168.
36. Frost, The Notebooks, ix.
37. Carver, "Rewilding . . . Conservation and Conflict," 2.
38. Smith, "Frost on the Apple," 691.
39. Klein, "The Counterlove of Robert Frost," 366.
40. Klein, 372.
41. Frost, A Boy's Will, 48–49.
42. Frost, New Hampshire, 15.
43. Frost, The Collected Prose, 131.
44. Frost, 132.
45. Watson, "'New Terms of Worth,'" 335.
46. Frost, The Collected Prose, 131.
47. Frost, New Hampshire, 50.
48. Frost, 88.
49. Frost, The Collected Prose, 132.
50. Klein, "The Counterlove of Robert Frost," 372.
51. Schroeder, "Andrew Wyeth and the Transcendental Tradition," 560–61.
52. Link, "Nature's Extra-Vagrants," 183.
53. Dickey, "Frost's 'The Tuft of Flowers,'" 299.
54. Klein, "The Counterlove of Robert Frost," 362.
55. Frost, North of Boston, 10.
56. Klein, "The Counterlove of Robert Frost," 370.
57. Zapf, Literature as Cultural Ecology, 171.
58. Cooper, "Robert Frost and Modernism," 89.
59. Levin, "Robert Frost and Pragmatism," 140.

60. Watson, "'New Terms of Worth,'" 316.
61. Mannon, "Georgic Environmentalism in North of Boston," 346.
62. Mannon, 348.
63. Mannon, 359.
64. Frost, *New Hampshire*, 14.
65. Frost, *Mountain Interval*, 58.
66. Frost, *Robert Frost*, 242.
67. Zapf, *Literature as Cultural Ecology*, 3.
68. Guha, "A Century of Dying," 306–7.
69. Eisenberg, "Rewilding Thinking," 48.
70. Guha, "A Century of Dying," 307.
71. "Returning Native Plants to the Maine Landscape."
72. "Rewild."
73. "Rewilding."
74. "Rewilding."
75. "Our Core Values."
76. "Returning Native Plants to the Maine Landscape."
77. "Rewilding Glossary."
78. "Returning Native Plants to the Maine Landscape."
79. The National Broadcasting Company, "A Conversation with Robert Frost," 3:03.
80. Frost, *New Hampshire*, 16.

A Review of *Old Poets:*
Reminiscences & Opinions

Donald Hall, *Old Poets: Reminiscences & Opinions* (Boston: Godine, 2021).

Reviewed by Henry Wise, Virginia Military Institute

All too often, we are taught to revere poets as monuments, but rarely do we have an opportunity to see them as people who struggled to live and write the poems we read and love. Donald Hall's *Old Poets: Reminiscences & Opinions* provides insight into the character and personality of some of the key figures in twentieth-century poetry. Published in its first iteration in 1978 as *Remembering Poets*, and again with additional material in 1992 as *Their Ancient Glittering Eyes*, this new version marks a forty-year period of continued reflection and revision, a project that occupied in some measure the latter half of Donald Hall's life. In this edition, the author recalls his relationships and interactions with Robert Frost, Dylan Thomas, T. S. Eliot, Archibald MacLeish, Yvor Winters, Marianne Moore, and Ezra Pound. Hall, whose life spanned from 1928 to 2018, is uniquely positioned to relay these memoirs about a transition from modernism to postmodernism, and does so in a manner both scholars and general readers will find rewarding. With the critical poetic eye of a writer and academic, *Old Poets* looks at these figureheads with patient curiosity and admiration, sharing with the reader a rare and intimate look at literary icons whose lives are little known apart from anecdotal gossip.

In fact, Hall attempts to calibrate the reader's expectations by claiming his book is mere gossip: "I do not speak of literary biography, a scholar's task, but of literary gossip, reminiscences by friends and acquaintances of authors" (3). However, he does himself a slight disservice as the book accomplishes more than gossip can. Though there is indeed an informality in his observations, he employs a poet's observational skills and an academic's analysis when considering his subjects. Despite the widespread tendency to disregard the author in favor of the work, Hall states, "if we admire the poem, it is natural to be curious about the poet" (5). In his short preface, "A Poet's Education," which precedes Hall's introduction, Wesley McNair exposes the underlying earnestness of the author: "Hall was so devoted to the work of the subjects in this book that he'd learned many of their poems by heart, yet the brilliance of these essays is how Hall keeps poetry in reserve, deploying it at exactly the right moment to enforce the points he makes" (XIX). *Old Poets* does more than recollect; it often leads to surprising epiphanies and profound insights drawn from experience.

Hall introduces *Old Poets* by acknowledging some ambivalence in "associat[ing] my name with the old poets whom I knew so little" (6). But he turns insecurity into determination: "Yet I feel no shame. This book records a portion of my education" (6). The poets about whom he writes are a part of his own story. Though they taught him "nothing directly about my own work . . . Instead of advice, they provided the gift of their existence and endurance" (6). Hall seems throughout *Old Poets* to suggest that we learn from others as much as we learn from their accomplishments, and we gain his perspectives as a younger poet looking ahead ("their presences glittered for me. . . . Their presences have been emblems of my life, and I remember these poets as if I kept them carved in stone" [13]) as well as an established one looking back.

Hall's first chapter, "Vanity, Fame, Love, and Robert Frost," analyzes an evolving relationship shared with Frost over several decades. In a way, this chapter sets the tone for the book. He begins by discussing the various versions of Frost, ranging from benign to monstrous, ending with the observation that controls the chapter: "Over the years he changed, for me, from a monument to a public fraud to something more human and complicated than either" (16). In a sense, this underscores one of the dominant themes of the book: that the gods and goddesses of poetry are complex individuals. He depicts Frost as a man with a conviction that he was deserving of the trials he and his family endured—including death, poverty, and suicide—for which he felt he was to blame. Hall's handling of such various sides to Frost and the other poets is valuable because it indicates some of the compulsion to write. In Frost's case, it helps explain his need for a forgiveness in the purity inherent in poetry. As Hall states, "He was vain, he could be cruel, he was rivalrous with all other men; but he could also be generous and warm—when he could satisfy himself that his motives were dubious. He was a man possessed by guilt, by knowledge that he was *bad*, by the raving for love and the necessity to reject love offered— and by desire for fame that no amount of celebrity could satisfy" (16).

Frost's idiosyncrasies are perhaps most apparent in his surprising penchant for performance. Hall concludes that Frost "*performed* in order to be *loved*" (25). This insight is later echoed in the author's observations of T. S. Eliot's deep insecurities that appear in his poetry and the "fragments" of Ezra Pound in his later years. To return to Frost, Hall observes, "The need for love and applause was a need for forgiveness" (27). And yet, tragically, the consolation of being absolved seemed impossible: "Frost felt guilty every minute he lived, and sought forgiveness everywhere and accepted none of it" (18).

Hall aptly places Frost as a conservative outlier among others of his period, pointing out a personal and political counterpoint: Ezra Pound. "Pound was champion of modernism and free verse, while Frost wrote sonnets and took every occasion to ridicule verse without meter" (31). One comes to understand, through Donald Hall's interpretation of Frost's poetry (particularly "Out, Out—"), that the man created an immortal, pure art from a very flawed and human need. One of the more surprising themes of the chapter on Frost is that of patriotism. When considering Ezra Pound's support of Mussolini, Hall, by comparison, references Frost's traditionally patriotic views. This will perhaps not surprise Frost's readers. Much like his poetry, Frost stays firmly planted in the American soil, deriving his unique and more subtly innovative voice from the material that inspired another bard of the nation: Walt Whitman.

Hall's experiences with Robert Frost, which continued through the end of Frost's life, give us a valuable perspective of a complex individual propelled by ambition and pain. In our current milieu of labels and tags that reduce public figures to words and phrases, Hall's observations of Frost and others are most welcome. Rather than attempting to sum up the poet of legendary fame, Hall presents him and the other subjects in this book as flawed individuals capable of greatness, skillfully removing himself from judging them while giving himself the freedom to observe. Our appreciation of poetry should not be confined to biography, but it certainly enhances the understanding of it. Hall leaves us the sense that we have been privileged to share in greatness, to get to know the individuals who became icons, and that this is perhaps the best way of honoring them. It would seem that honoring them might indeed be the point of the book: "Whatever old poets feel as they come toward the end of their lives, they have spent their lives trying to make antidotes to death; we honor this making when we attend to their lives and characters" (13). In *Old Poets*, Donald Hall gives us a link to the past, and he also exemplifies his own relevance as an old poet, flawed and capable of greatness, a guide for poets to come.

A REVIEW OF *RHYME'S ROOMS: THE ARCHITECTURE OF POETRY*

Brad Leithauser, *Rhyme's Rooms: The Architecture of Poetry* (New York: Alfred A. Knopf, 2022).

Reviewed by A. M. Juster

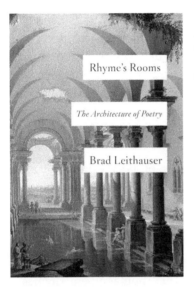

Even a poetry lover might question the need for yet another book for people eager to write poetry. Members of the free verse literary establishment have written many such books without any particular one becoming preeminent. When it comes to formal poetry, these works either ignore traditional prosody or discuss it quickly and inaccurately. For literary holdouts, there is the consolation that we have had for several decades two outstanding books about writing poetry in rhyme and meter: Timothy Steele's *All the Fun's in How You Say a Thing* and William Baer's *Writing Metrical Poetry.*

The literary allegiances of Brad Leithauser, the author of *Rhyme's Rooms,* should be clear from his book's title, but his background makes it extremely clear. Leithauser, despite being (as I am) a graduate of Harvard Law School, has been one of the most distinguished members of the New Formalism literary movement that caught fire after Dana Gioia's 1991 "Can Poetry Matter?" essay in the *Atlantic Monthly.* Leithauser's formal poetry predated Gioia's essay; his 1982 debut book *Hundreds of Fireflies* attracted considerable attention for its formal bent, and he went on to publish nine more books of poetry as well as a verse novel, prose novels, and literary criticism. He recently retired after many years as a professor at Johns Hopkins, which I consider the country's top writing program.

While many poets claim that the constraints of formal poetry inhibit creativity, Robert Frost always argued that such constraints actually spur creativity. Leithauser's career provides ample evidence for this effect, perhaps most amusingly in his raunchy monometer sonnet, "Post-Coitum Tristesse: A Sonnet."

Leithauser brings that same kind of creativity and humor to *Rhyme's Rooms* (a title which is a "rim rhyme," as is "rim rhyme" itself), particularly in the unusual and savvy way that he defines his mission. This book occupies largely virgin territory because its target audience is neither the person who knows little or nothing about poetry, nor the person who has decided to write formal poetry. His book aims, instead, for "the reader who loves words and literature but maybe feels some trepidation and a little nervous resentment, as well as various unvoiced cravings, on confronting a poem on the page." Given how shoddily higher education teaches poetry these days, Leithauser has no shortage of potential readers.

Rhyme's Rooms explains techniques of poetry in a clear and accurate fashion while also trying to excite readers about the many uses for those techniques. The book's palpable enthusiasm for subjects that many find tedious goes a long way to helping it to make its case.

The book begins with a whimsical thought experiment that contrasts the rhyme of Dylan Thomas's "Prologue" with the rhyme of Robert Frost's "After Apple-Picking." The Thomas poem rhymes its first and hundredth lines, and the rhymes approach the middle of the poem unheard until they finally reach a few lines in its center, which leads Leithauser to a discussion of the limits on our ability to hear rhyme. In contrast, the Frost poem has "clangorous" rhymes in its early lines, but then Frost muffles his rhyming to create the sobering effect that his story demands.

In the following chapter Leithauser, still obviously not fully shaking his legal training, lays out his book's central theme: "the prosodic contract"—in other words, the expectations that a poet creates with his use of words early in a poem:

A formal poem presents its potential reader with a deal, offer, exchange, pact. The centrality of this deal, often remarkable for its specificity, is what most decisively distinguishes verse from prose, the overall experience of a formal poem from that of a piece of fiction or a creative essay. I call this deal or exchange the prosodic contract. (16)

He then correctly notes that most formal poems satisfy the expectations created by their prosodic contracts and acknowledges that such fulfillment is often a source of satisfaction, as when other kinds of contracts deliver what is expected. Importantly, though, he does not stop there, and through close readings of poems by Elizabeth Bishop, Philip Larkin, and others, he demonstrates how "infringing" reasonable reader expectations (there's that law school training again...) can elevate the art of a poem. He also uses poems by Frost and Richard Wilbur to analyze how poets "loosen" the prosodic contract and how a few highly skilled poets adhere to their prosodic contracts while still managing to catch the reader off-guard with their prosody.

By this point, Leithauser has established the terms of *his* contract with the readers of this book. Chapters 3–20 skillfully, and often humorously, address mostly predictable elements of traditional prosody, such as stanzas, iambic meters, and enjambment. There are also seven chapters dealing with issues relating to rhyme. Since there have been few thorough discussions of rhyme in recent decades, these chapters offer readers the greatest value. There are also a few chapters devoted to more unlikely topics, such as song lyrics, wordplay, and the look of a poem on the page.

The style of most of these chapters also establishes contractual expectations. Chapters usually start with a description of the topic, and then are followed by analyses enhanced with close readings of such icons of formal poetry as Frost, Wilbur, Larkin, and Bishop. Leithauser does occasionally include surprises, such as his fondness for the syllabics of Marianne Moore and his appreciation for wondrous but obscure contemporary poets like Bill Coyle. He does not focus exclusively on formal poetry and will point out how the kind of craft he is discussing can enhance free verse as well. He even surprises his core audience on occasion, as when he deftly skewers a popular New Formalist theory that a love of meter is biologically based.

These discussions avoid the labored pomposities of the academy. His style is breezily plain-spoken, and his asides often include his best insights. After a while, the reader's experience starts to feel somewhat like sitting long ago cross-legged in a college courtyard listening to the cool, smart professor who is on a roll.

Leithauser infringes his own contract a bit at the end but does not inflict any harm by doing so. The final five chapters have a bit of the feel of a litigator's closing argument, and for the most part he repeats and amplifies points he has made before—although his brilliant chapter on the difficult prosody of Gerard Manley Hopkins is unexpected and by itself worth the price of the book.

Leithauser seems to have a clear eye for the profile of his audience: "Poetry's openness to eccentrics and cranks and misfits fosters a landscape remarkable for its extreme features. It revels in queer contours, harsh outcroppings, pointed unlovelinesses. Not surprisingly, its inhabitants are frequently opinionated and uncentered and off-putting" (332). In light of this assessment, he should not be surprised that this opinionated and off-putting lover of prosody, who has been known to enjoy heated late-night debates about whether spondees actually exist, has a few picky reservations about his book. For instance, I thought it odd that the book's discussions of sonnets never used the phrase "Petrarchan sonnet," but used instead "Miltonic sonnet." Milton's sonnets were highly derivative of Petrarch's and significantly less influential—and the Miltonic sonnet as Leithauser uses the term is essentially interchangeable with the Petrarchan sonnet. It would have been more helpful to readers for him to tip the hat in the more deserving direction.

I loved much of the chapter on song lyrics and will never think about the words of Paul McCartney's "Yesterday" in the same way, but the section on humorous lyrics did suffer a bit from its failure to mention the great Tom Lehrer, for instance, or amazing musicians who came into their prime after the breakup of The Beatles, most notably Warren Zevon, Lin-Manuel Miranda, and Richard Thompson. These flaws are minor, however, and my harshest criticism of the book is reserved for the unnamed editor at Knopf who made the shortsighted and undoubtedly budget-driven decision not to include an index. *Rhyme's Rooms* is loaded with valuable information and pithy quotations to which many readers will want to return. Given the book's length and the author's penchant for wonderful digressions and asides, it will often be difficult for a reader to find vaguely remembered wisdom. Regrettably, this shortcoming means the book will be cited less often, and thus Knopf will sell fewer books than it should.

These concerns do not undermine my opinion that *Rhyme's Rooms* is a terrific and unique book that does more to help would-be poets who are anxious about "confronting a poem on the page" than the scores of currently available guides for the perplexed.

A Review of *Robert Frost's Visionary Gift: Mining and Minding the Wonder of Unexpected Supply*

William F. Zak, *Robert Frost's Visionary Gift: Mining and Minding the Wonder of Unexpected Supply* (Lanham, MD: Lexington Books, 2022)

Reviewed by John Gatta, The University of the South, Sewanee

For decades now, the elevated schoolroom reputation of Robert Frost as a favored, unusually accessible, and quotable American poet has endured with little pause. Among all other modern poets, his esteem in that sphere remains unsurpassed. But his critical rank has rarely won him so high a standing. Does Frost's literary achievement really display enough artistry, gravitas, and scope to warrant placing him within the pantheon of modernist figures like Yeats and Eliot?

For William Zak, the answer is unequivocally "yes," and by virtue of this well-informed, cogently argued volume, bolstered with an array of close readings, he makes good on his claim for Frost as a visionary and philosophic poet of the highest order. Having previously published on Shakespeare, Zak here displays a thorough acquaintance with Frost's prose and poetic writings, together with the relevant biographical and contextual underpinnings of this corpus. *Robert Frost's Visionary Gift* brings this knowledge effectively to bear as it addresses several theoretical dimensions of the poet's achievement, especially in its opening chapters, while supplying in its middle and latter chapters an abundance of practical criticism.

A leading contention of this book is that Frost deserves to be taken more seriously than commonly recognized as a relentlessly philosophic poet and a penetrating "spirit guide." The particular aspect of philosophic discernment Zak attributes to the poet strikes me as more nearly ethical than metaphysical—that is, as casting light upon the question of how then we shall live, in the given world we inhabit. Zak does not understand this visionary charism of the poet to offer any definitive statement about life's ultimate meaning. The "modest guiding light" (x) it offers can nonetheless lead us toward finding a "place among infinities" ("The Star Splitter") capable of redeeming our otherwise desperate state of neediness in this fallen world. Its wisdom, in other words, enlightens our way toward apprehending at least some "momentary stay against confusion"—to invoke a classic Frostian motto—but no permanent rest from our existential terror.

In this portrayal, Frost also figures as a prophetic descendent of such kindred spirits as Wordsworth and Thoreau, with their Romantic ideals reconfigured to suit a modernist, more colloquialized context. Much as Wordsworth, in the light of common day, had reenvisioned Milton's land of promise as a "Paradise within," so also Frost becomes "the latest prophetic descendant and seer of this Romantic visionary ideal" (xi).

Through his detailed and often demanding exposition, Zak makes a compelling case in support of each of these claims. What I value most in the book, though, are its commentaries on individual poems. Zak incorporates into his treatment a wealth of close readings, including readings of less-known pieces such as "On a Tree Fallen Across the Road" and "The Tuft of Flowers." For me, this volume's most memorable reassessments are of poems I had known and read for years, taught now and then to students, and thought I understood. *Thought* I understood—but had never apprehended as fully as they deserved. The eye-opening interpretations Zak supplies for these "magisterially memorable lyrics" (236) are well worth the volume's purchase. That favored list includes old chestnuts such as "Birches," "Mending Wall," "The Wood-Pile," "Design," "After Apple-Picking," and "The Need of Being Versed in Country Things." It includes as well brilliant readings of two of Frost's dramatic narratives: "The Death of the Hired Man" and "Home Burial."

On a couple of points, I believe Zak's arguments could use refinement or qualification. He suggests, for example, that Frost's overall accomplishment as a spirit guide ranks him not only *among* modernism's leading poets of the twentieth century, but at the very head of that distinguished company. "Frost's importance as a poetic visionary," he contends, "soars well beyond (and more widely and circumspectly than) anything that his poetic contemporaries accomplished, however brightly they, too, shone" (17). Such judgments are largely, to be sure, a matter of personal taste. But Zak's claim for the singular merit of Frost's wisdom, over against that of an Eliot or Yeats or Stevens, risks turning what I take to be modernism's convocation of voices into a needless competition. For me nothing in Frost's poetic corpus, for all its revelatory worth, quite eclipses the momentous scale and impact of what Eliot has left us in works such as *The Waste Land* or *Four Quartets*. Zak's lofty general claims for Frost as poet-prophet also seem to contradict this critic's otherwise sound emphasis on the understated, modest force of the guidance available to us across the span of Frost's lyrics.

Another limitation sometimes discernible in Zak's approach has to do with how we are to discern, in particular cases, the relation between the poet and his fictive persona. Characteristically, Zak perceives in his reading of Frostian lyrics more ironic distance between the speaker and the poet in person than most interpreters are inclined to grant. This approach often serves Zak well. I find it persuasively applied, for example, throughout his commentary on "The Need of Being Versed in Country Things." There he underscores "the distance between the heartening song of the phoebes" and "the disheartened lament sung by the persona." Thus pointing out the "arbitrary anthropomorphism" displayed by the persona, he ends up suggesting how "Frost identifies himself even more with the phoebes who 'rejoiced in the nest they kept' than with the hapless melancholy of the persona who deplores them while he dwells alone and 'too much' on the ashes of the ruinous spectacle before him" (340–41). Such a reading offers fresh insight into this familiar poem.

In other cases, though, Zak's inclination to perceive a great gulf fixed between poet and persona strikes me as problematic. That's so in the book's closing chapter, for example, where Zak's somewhat convoluted reading of "Directive" aims to make coherent sense of a poem that seems to defy all forms of coherent explication. Up to a point, Zak's distancing from the sage impression of that poem's final lines seems apt, as does his emphasis on Frost's "deflation of our gullibly roused hopes" (378). However, how much of the speaker's discourse in "Directive" we are to take ironically strikes me as an unsettled and perhaps unsolvable enigma.

The major strength of *Robert Frost's Visionary Gift* lies in its close readings, which are often penetrating and always pursued with diligence and intelligence. But the book also contains a number of worthwhile theoretical reflections—on topics such as the limits of intellection, Frost's mythopoetic vision of pastoral, the usual indifference of the natural order to human sensibilities, and, in biographical perspective, the poet's often troubled relation to his rural neighbors. Above all, it probes with grace and rigor the existential question of how we might, as votaries of Frost's spirit guidance, better learn to discover "our place among infinities."

A Review of *American Wildflowers: A Literary Field Guide*

Susan Barba, editor; Leanne Shapton, illustrator, *American Wildflowers: A Literary Field Guide* (New York: Abrams, 2022)

Reviewed by Owen Sholes, Assumption College

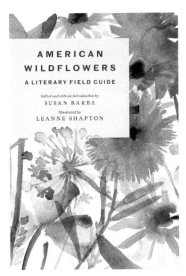

Susan Barba has compiled an anthology of writings by a diverse collection of authors as a guide to some of the wildflowers of North America. The anthology includes 101 selections by eighty-five writers, all of which include one or more types of North American wildflowers in some way. There is one poem by Robert Frost ("An Encounter") that ends with the line "Half looking for the orchid Calypso." It is that wild orchid that justifies the inclusion of the poem in this anthology.

Barba invited Leanne Shapton to illustrate the flowers and the writings. Shapton's watercolors are colorful and suggestive, without the precision of botanical illustration but with a vitality that complements the writing. Her paintings of goldenrods, for example (some of which I have studied), are simple, bright, and essential. Overall, the colors of the flowers are often vivid, sometimes morose, sometimes not matching the actual flowers. The shapes range from crisp to imprecise, realistic to impressionistic. There is always some connection to the flowers as they occur in the wild, but the closeness of those connections varies widely.

Barba set out to reveal a literature of North American wildflowers that had previously been lacking or unrecognized. She chose writings from various perspectives, genres, and purposes, and assembled them alphabetically by formal names of the plant families, ending with a catchall of generic wildflowers. The diversity of authors, in every sense of that term, results in a multifaceted anthology connected by the unifying theme of wildflowers. The authors are or were well established, published, and often recognized by awards for their work. These writers are not undiscovered talents, though the reader might discover them for the first time. Essentially any reader should find something familiar and something new. Best of all, Barba has succeeded in revealing that there is a multifaceted literature of wildflowers. With their appetites whetted, readers can explore these authors in more detail, and see what else lies within the dozen recommendations for further reading.

Barba's goal is to create biographies of wildflowers, not botanies. While there is some explicit botany in the collection (Thomas Jefferson specifically instructed Meriwether Lewis to describe new plant species), I think that the works are more like profiles than biographies. The profiles are inevitably inconsistent among varied pieces, and even the broadest coverage is, in works so short, incomplete. But they are an interesting and engaging start.

Shapton's paintings, in contrast to the writing, are much closer to biography, letting each plant show something of itself, if only through a human brush. In her notes about the illustrations, Shapton hopes that readers will pick flowers and press them in this book, perhaps because the pigments will bleed into the pages, adding their own art. Other writers make other suggestions. In apposition to the table of contents, Katie Peterson writes that she will "make a bouquet," a task that will require picking flowers. Then the introduction quotes Edna St. Vincent Millay: "I will touch a hundred flowers / And not pick one." Neltje Blanchan scolds merchants and collectors for picking huge quantities of trailing arbutus, a plant that grows only in the wild. Katherine White notes cultural differences in picking flowers: Japanese children, she tells us, do not automatically pick flowers, but American children often do (yes, including trailing arbutus). Eleanor Perenyi has occasionally dug up wildflowers to plant on her own property, but only if they are abundant (or threatened with imminent destruction), and only if she knows they will survive. The ultimate decision to pick, or not, is thus left to the reader.

By presenting the works according to plant family, Barba gives the plants top billing, even if the alphabet puts unrelated families close together. This organization makes each family easy to find. The names of the families and species are those widely accepted by the botanical community (and sometimes different from those I learned decades ago in my formal training). There is no author index, so a reader must scan six pages of contents to find a particular writer. (Short biographies are included alphabetically at the end, a nice addition.) There is no list of genre, geography, gender, ethnicity, or date; these are things for the reader to discover along any chosen path through the anthology.

The formality of the botanical names is tempered by the presence of common names. Thus, the book is aimed at a general reader, anyone who wants to explore facets of the lives of these plants, and to become familiar with plant lives, even if they have never seen the plants themselves. Having almost entirely avoided technical writing, Barba has made the collection accessible to nearly anyone.

There are two conspicuous formatting errors. Two lines of "Spring and All" by William Carlos Williams are repeated on consecutive pages, and the last twenty lines of "The Message" by Denise Levertov are missing.

What should a reader expect from an anthology? Such collections long predate today's playlists but provide the same introduction to things that readers might not discover on their own. If chosen well, as in this anthology, each piece will have an intensity that makes the reader take notice. Then the reader can decide how to react. Barba sought "radically decentering texts," and for the most part succeeded. Reading these authors is indeed a decentering experience because each is so different, and each one is deeply intent on telling a story or imparting information.

There is always the theme: wildflowers. There is joy of discovery of wildflowers; despair over flowers being destroyed; flowers as the décor for mourning, or celebration, or ritual; investigation of flowers never seen before; preparation for finding flowers and turning them into food; anticipation when there are only seeds of flowers in winter. Going from piece to piece, the reader encounters new voices, new intentions, new moods, and new species. Readers can make their own path through the collection, and any path will be enlightening.

Unrestricted by genre, wildflowers are present in every selection, sometimes beginning to end, sometimes just one species, sometimes a multitude. Sometimes flowers are the central message, sometimes only in support of another topic, sometimes just a glancing reference that might be missed if we didn't know there had to be a flower in there, somewhere.

Frost's "An Encounter" is one of the poems that barely mentions flowers. The encounter is not with a flower but with a utility pole, a log raised upright to support wires. The narrator is taking a break from his difficult hike through a cedar bog and ponders the significance of this pole, the transmissions through its wires, and his own meanderings through the countryside. "Calypso" is the last word of the poem, the name of an orchid he might encounter. But this afterthought is in the perfect position to send the reader scurrying to another source to see what the Calypso orchid is. One hopes that the search is rewarded with any illustration of its beautiful flower. No wonder the wanderer of the poem is hoping to find this plant in bloom.

Barba's volume includes one other connection to Frost, though it is probably unintentional. Among the list of "Further Reading" is *How to Know the Wild Flowers* by Mrs. William Starr Dana, a book that Frost claimed to have carried with him on many of his early botanizing walks. This book is still in print and contains stories and histories about the flowers it includes. To some degree, Dana's book is an early contribution to the literature of North American wildflowers, a precursor to Barba's anthology.

If someone wanted to compile a literature of North American wildflowers exclusively from the work of Robert Frost, there are at least twenty families of flowers included in his poetry, representing about thirty species (plus others unspecified, as in "The Last Mowing": "All shapes and colors of flowers, / I needn't call you by name"). The anthology would not be as varied as Barba's, but it might provide an interesting insight into Frost. Until a willing editor produces such a collection (I have no intention of doing so), any reader will find much to enjoy in Barba's anthology.

Recent Frost Scholarship

Books

Zak, William F. *Robert Frost's Visionary Gift: Mining and Minding the Wonder of Unexpected Supply*. Lanham: Rowman & Littlefield, 2022.

Book chapters

Charlwood, Catherine. "Corresponding Listeners: Walter de La Mare and Robert Frost." In *Walter de La Mare: Critical Appraisals*, edited by Yui Kajita, Angela Leighton, and A. J. Nickerson, 43–60. Liverpool: Liverpool University Press, 2022.

Paeth, Amy. "Epilogue: 'An Invisible Berlin Wall,' the U.S. Inaugural Poem, and the Future of State Verse." In *The American Poet Laureate: A History of U.S. Poetry and the State*, 192–208. New York: Columbia University Press, 2023.

———. "Inaugurating National Poetry: Robert Frost and Cold War Arts, 1956–1965." In *The American Poet Laureate: A History of U.S. Poetry and the State*, 63–99. New York: Columbia University Press, 2023.

Perelman, Bob. "On Robert Frost, 'Mending Wall' (1914)." In *The Difference Is Spreading: Fifty Contemporary Poets on Fifty Poems*, edited by Al Filreis and Anna Strong Safford, 18–22. Philadelphia: University of Pennsylvania Press, 2022.

Post, Jonathan F. S. "Frost in the Company of Shakespeare and Wordsworth." In *The American Sonnet: An Anthology of Poems and Essays*, edited by Dora Malech and Laura T. Smith, 260–66. Iowa City: University of Iowa Press, 2022.

Dissertations

Carte, Donald Thomas. "Diverging in the Woods: The Journeys of Robert Frost and T.S. Eliot to WWI England and the Impact on Fashioning Two Distinct Poetic Identities." PhD diss., Harvard University, 2022.

Martin, Ryan. "Music Inspired by the Works of Robert Frost." PhD diss., University of Arkansas, 2022. [PhD in music composition; consists of musical scores.]

Interview

Yezzi, David. "Gordon Clapp and Tom Durham: Playing Thomas, Playing Frost." *Robert Frost Review*, no. 32 (2022): 101–16.

Journal Articles

Barron, Jonathan N. "New Hampshire's Secret Modernism: 'For Once, Then, Something.'" *Robert Frost Review*, no. 32 (2022): 55–74.

Davis, Matthew M. "'The Wood Wakes': Robert Frost's 'A Dream Pang' and the Aubade Tradition." *Robert Frost Review*, no. 32 (2022): 75–88.

Davoudian, Armen. "Robert Frost: Poems in Books, Poems against Books." *Modern Philology* 120, no. 4 (May 2023): 497–522.

O'Brien, Timothy. "Another Shaker of Salt: 'To Earthward.'" *ANQ: A Quarterly Journal of Short Articles, Notes & Reviews* 36, no. 2 (April 2023): 240–42.

Rahimtoola, Samia. "Ruin Gazing: Robert Frost and the Afterlives of Settler Environmentalism." *The Yearbook of Comparative Literature* 64 (2022): 144–71.

Werner, Maximilian. "Walking the Line: 'Mending Wall' as *Ars Poetica*." *Robert Frost Review*, no. 32 (2022): 89–98.

Wolfson, Susan J. "Robert Frost: Teaching and the Pleasure of Ulteriority." *Essays in Criticism* 73, no. 1 (January 2023): 53–75.

Notes

Abrams, Douglas E. "References to Robert Frost's Poetry in Advocacy and Judicial Opinions." *Journal of the Missouri Bar* 78, no. 5 (September 2022): 237–38.

Belkora, Leila. "Astronomical, Meteorological, and Optical Effects in 'Iris by Night.'" *Robert Frost Review*, no. 32 (2022): 39–52.

———. "The Historical Context of Robert Frost's Enthusiasm for Astronomy." *Robert Frost Review*, no. 32 (2022): 25–38.

Fan, Weina. "The Lacanian Subject in Robert Frost's 'The Road Not Taken.'" *Explicator* 80, no. 3/4 (July 2022): 81–85.

Kim, Wook-Dong. "'Stopping by Woods on a Snowy Evening': Robert Frost's Comments on Emerson." *ANQ: A Quarterly Journal of Short Articles, Notes & Reviews* (May 2023): 1–4. doi:10.1080/0895769x.2023.2210175.

Kuttappan, Joy, and Gauri Joy. "Obscure Biblical Allusions in Robert Frost's 'Mending Wall.'" *Human Behavior, Development &*

Society 24, no. 1 (January 2023): 93–101.

Thornton, Jack. "Robert Frost's Key West Cottage: Another Roadside Attraction." *Robert Frost Review*, no. 32 (2022): 11–24.

Review

Steinhafel, John Matthew. "'All the Fun's in How You Say a Thing': Performing the Poetry of Robert Frost." *Robert Frost Review*, no. 32 (2022): 117–124.

In Memoriam – Robert N. Ganz Jr.

Foreword by Lesley L. Francis

While it saddens me personally to accept the passing of our dear friend Bob Ganz, I am one of those fortunate enough to have enjoyed more than twenty-six years listening to Bob contribute to the open discussions at the many annual Robert Frost Symposia. He never failed to stimulate our appreciation of Frost the poet and of his deeply Emersonian philosophy. When he and I met, I soon learned that my mother, sister, Elinor, and I had been close neighbors of Ganz and his family on Brown Street in Cambridge, not long before the poet began what would be a lifelong relationship with Amherst College, and where today the library bears his name. It is only fitting that our lives would overlap. I am indeed honored to add my name to those who were to get to know Bob at George Washington University in Washington, DC, or at the family's home in Martha's Vineyard.

What follows is taken from the well-expressed obituary provided by his family, and parts of which published at the time of his death in the *Martha's Vineyard Times*. I believe it conveys a warm appreciation of Bob's personality, intellect, and love of family and friends.

Bob and Anne Ganz celebrating their 50th wedding anniversary
(Courtesy of the Ganz family.)

One of Robert Ganz Jr.'s most cherished keepsakes was a holograph of the poem "Peril of Hope" that Robert Frost wrote out for him at his home on Brewster Street in Cambridge in April 1962. Bob was fond of pointing out that it contained different wording from the version Frost published that same year in the volume *In the Clearing*. Bob's copy reads:

It's right in there
Betwixt and between
The orchard bare
And the orchard green,
There's a coming out
of flowery promise
I have to doubt
As a doubting Thomas.
For it's overdone
It seems possessed
By spring and sun –
And bees the rest
And there's not a clime
But for all the cost
Will take that time
For a night of frost.

Signed "Robert Frost, For Robert Ganz, Brewster Village, April 3, 1962."

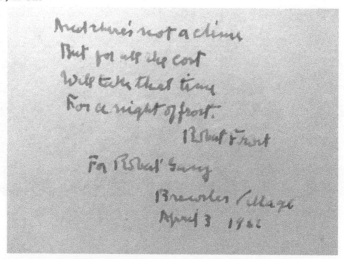

Detail from Frost inscription of "Peril of Hope" in the cover of Bob's copy of *In the Clearing*. (Courtesy of the Ganz family.)

Years later, also in April, Bob's family would be reminded of the fragility of hope in early spring, when, after a brief rally, he lost his battle with sarcoma.

Bob died at home in Chilmark, Massachusetts, on April 9, 2023, at the age of ninety-seven. A World War II veteran and professor emeritus at George Washington University, he had been a seasonal resident of Martha's Vineyard since 1938, before moving with his wife, Anne Hotchkiss Ganz, to the island permanently in 2013.

Born in Boston, Bob grew up in Cambridge, Massachusetts. According to family lore, as a young boy, the future professor would sometimes stand on an ash barrel outside the house his parents first rented at 16 Brown St., giving soapbox style speeches to anyone who would listen. He spoke with what he called "a regional accent," a now possibly extinct form of New England drawl that young Bobby (which he pronounced "Bahh-bay") honed in the schoolyards of Cambridge in the 1920s and '30s (where, it seemed, competing accents could vary from block to block). He attended the recently founded Cambridge Nursery School on Avon Hill, with his lifelong friend Robert Freeman Whitman, also a future English professor. The two went on to Browne and Nichols School, where both graduated from high school in 1943. Bob then matriculated at Harvard College as a member of the class of 1947. After one semester, he volunteered for the Army, and served as a rifleman with the 10th Mountain Division ("the ski troops") during World War II. He was wounded in Italy at the age of nineteen, just two weeks before the German Army's surrender. He received the Bronze Star, two Battle Stars, and the Purple Heart.

On the afternoon of April 17, 1945, Bob's platoon came under "machine gun, mortar, and artillery fire" from Nazi German defenses, as they moved toward a fellow company fighting for Mount Serra in northern Italy (according to George F. Earle's "History of the 87th Mountain Infantry in Italy 1945"). "They were able," the account continues, "to keep moving until two or three hundred yards from the houses beyond La Ca. Here a machine gun opened up on the platoon, after allowing the scouts, runner, platoon leader, and four men of the 3rd Squad to go by. The platoon lay flat in the tall grass, unable to move. Only those men without packs were safe, as the bullets mowed across the grass tops. Pfc. Manfred Butler was fatally hit in the neck by machine gun fire, and Pfc. Robert N. Ganz Jr. was wounded as his rifle grenade was detonated." The rest of his division would break through German defenses that day, and be in position to advance subsequently to the Po River Valley. (Germany would officially surrender in Italy on May 2.)

Bob was left with battle scars on his knee and abdomen and retained shrapnel for the rest of his life. His son once remarked he could be proud of the fact he was wounded in his front, facing the enemy, not his back. But Bob urged his children to be cautious when talking about war and patriotism because many had died for the American flag (including Bob's best friend, Peter Powers, killed during the Battle of the Bulge). He mainly agreed with Benjamin Franklin, whose wit he admired, that, "there never was a good war or a bad peace."

After the war, Bob returned to Harvard, where he graduated in 1949 with an A.B. in American studies, and stayed on to complete his MA (in 1951) and PhD (in 1959) in English, studying the poetry of Robert Frost under professor Reuben A. Brower. His doctoral dissertation is titled "The Pattern of Meaning in Robert Frost's Poetry." In the middle 1950s, Bob was one of a number who enjoyed late-night exchanges with Frost in his cabin in Vermont. He said in the course of these conversations, "thought seemed to delight in its own spiraling expansion."

Bob would go on to write a book in 1968 titled *Robert Frost and the Play of Belief*, which was accepted for publication in both the US and the UK Cecil Day-Lewis, one of the directors of the London publishing house Chatto & Windus, would write to him that year: "I should have written to you a long time ago about your Frost book. But I have been living in a kind of pandemonium since my appointment two months ago, and am only just beginning to catch up with my work. I thought the book, in its revised form, was one of the very best critical studies I have ever read, and I am more than delighted that we are going to publish it. As I expect you know, we are in touch with your American publishers." However, in the end Bob modestly felt his work needed refinement, and pulled it from publication. He would continue to work on revising it for the rest of his life, including on Martha's Vineyard, where he would spend summer days reading in his barn and nights entertaining friends, including another Frost scholar, Stanley Burnshaw.

Bob met Anne Hotchkiss, then of West Tisbury, Massachusetts, in the summer of 1962. He began sailing on Martha's Vineyard with Anne and her brother, Henry. After an autumn of correspondence, their first date occurred when he invited her to Robert Frost's funeral in February 1963. Bob said afterward that Frost, as an ironist, would not have minded his funeral being the occasion for him to fall in love. He proposed to her on July 4 on top of "Proposal Hill" on Hollyholm, the family summer home, and they were married August 28, 1963, at the Old Whaling Church in Edgartown. When Bob passed away, he and Annie were in their sixtieth year of marriage.

Bob began teaching as an instructor at Yale before moving on to the University of Virginia, and finally settling at GWU in 1964. He came to GW as an Americanist with a special interest in twentieth-century American poetry. Having been broadly trained, he also taught the Great Books and European literature as the need arose within his department. He was pleased when a former student, Faye Moskowitz, went on to become the English department chair, and his boss. After fifty-plus years of teaching, he retired from GW when he was eighty-six years old, having taught more than three hundred fifty classes, and likely more than seven thousand students.

Bob was a frequent contributor to the annual RF Symposium, where he often enlightened scholars with his deep knowledge of how philosophers Henri Bergson and William James influenced Frost's habits of mind. Even after losing his eyesight, Ganz, with the guiding help of his daughter Claire, attended many of the symposia, where he cheerfully contributed personal anecdotes about his relationship with Frost and regaled colleagues with recitations of Frost's poetry.

After many years dividing their time between Washington, DC, and the family summer home, Anne and Bob moved to Chilmark to live year-round in 2013. Bob had long suspected that his better self lay beneath the leaves on Martha's Vineyard, as he put it.

Bob continued his Frost scholarship in his retirement. (Photo by Geoffrey Carter)

Bob was more interested in reading poetry than writing it. However, he once came up with the following verses while replacing window panes in his barn in Chilmark:

Puttying is like arguing.
Your touch has got to be soft.
Or else, when you think you're putting on,
You're really just putting off.

A scholarship fund for undergraduate English majors has been established in his honor at George Washington University.

For more information, please contact his family at ganzpoetry@gmail.com.

ENDNOTES

1 The version of the poem published in In the Clearing is only twelve lines long in three stanzas. The original can be found in *Robert Frost, Collected Poems, Prose & Plays*, edited by Richard Poirier and Mark Richardson (New York: Library of America, 1995), 455.

ABOUR OUR CONTRIBUTORS

ROBERT CRAWFORD is the director of poetry activities at the Robert Frost Farm. He is the author of two books of poetry, *The Empty Chair* (2011; recipient of the Richard Wilbur Award) and *Too Much Explanation Can Ruin a Man* (2005).

LESLEY LEE FRANCIS is the granddaughter of Robert Frost. She received her A.B. degree from Radcliffe College and her PhD in Romance Languages from Duke University. She has been a professor of Spanish language, literature, and history at several colleges and universities. She organized the Robert Frost Symposium from 1994 to 2019. Dr. Francis has lectured and published extensively on her grandfather. Her books include *Robert Frost: An Adventure in Poetry, 1900–1918* (2004) and *You Come Too: My Journey with Robert Frost* (2015).

JOHN GATTA is William R. Kenan Jr. Professor of English Emeritus at Sewanee, the University of the South, where he has also served as Dean of the College of Arts and Sciences. For much of his career, he taught at the University of Connecticut, Storrs. His scholarly publications have focused on American writing before 1900, with particular reference to environmental literature and the interplay between literary imagination and religious faith.

MARISSA GRUNES is a literary scholar and science writer focused on nineteenth-century American literature and visual culture, environmental history, and Antarctica. Her academic writing can be found in *Women's Studies*, *The Robert Frost Review*, and *Leviathan*, and she has published general readership articles in venues including *Atlas Obscura*, *Nautilus*, *The Paris Review Online*, *Connecticut Magazine*, and *The Conversation*. She is currently an instructor in the English Department at the University of Colorado, Boulder.

ROBERT BERNARD HASS is the executive director of the Robert Frost Society and a professor English at Penn West University of Pennsylvania. He is the author of *Going by Contraries: Robert Frost's Conflict with Science* (2002), a coeditor of the *Letters of Robert Frost*, Volumes 2 and 3 (2016, 2021), and the author of the poetry collection *Counting Thunder* (2008).

JAMES F. (JIM) HURLEY, a former business executive and corporate director, has contributed previously with "A Personal Rebuke from Robert Frost," his memoir of meeting Frost in April 1959 at the Iowa Writers Workshop. Hurley is the author of *A Westbound Sun*, a collection of poems, short stories, and memoirs. He is the Treasurer of the Robert Frost Society and, in 2019, led the establishment of the Society's permanent home at the San Diego Central Library.

A. M. JUSTER is the poetry editor for *Plough* and tweets profusely about formal poetry at @amjuster. His work has appeared in *Poetry*, *The Hudson Review*, and *The Paris Review*. His tenth book was *Wonder and Wrath* (2020); next year W. W. Norton will release his translation of Petrarch's *Canzoniere* and Paul Dry Books will release his first children's book, *Girlatee*.

KAREN L. KILCUP is the Elizabeth Rosenthal Excellence Professor of English, Environmental & Sustainability Studies, and Women's, Gender, & Sexuality Studies at UNC Greensboro. Kilcup's recent academic publications include *Who Killed American Poetry?: From National Obsession to Elite Possession* (2019) and *Stronger, Truer, Bolder: American Children's Writing, Nature, and the Environment* (2021). Her collection *The Art of Restoration* (2023) received the 2021 Winter Goose Poetry Prize, and her chapbook *Red Appetite* (2023) received the 2022 Helen Kay Chapbook Poetry Prize. Her forthcoming work includes a coedited volume, *The Selected Works of Ora Eddleman Reed: Author, Editor, and Activist for Cherokee Rights* (2024), and a second full-length poetry collection, *Feathers and Wedges*.

NANCY NAHRA has taught at the University of Vermont, at John Cabot University in Rome, and as Professor of Humanities at Champlain College, where she still occasionally teaches a literature course. Her poetry has won national awards. She writes scholarly articles and has coauthored four books. At present, she is living in Vermont and working on her forthcoming book on Robert Frost and classical authors.

ALEXANDRIA PEARY serves as New Hampshire Poet Laureate (2019-2024). She is the author of nine books, most recently *Battle of Silicon Valley at Daybreak* (2021) and *Prolific Moment: Theory and Practice of Mindfulness for Writing* (2018). She is the 2020 recipient of an Academy of American Poets Laureate Fellowship. She specializes in mindful writing, the subject of her 2019 TEDx talk, "How Mindfulness Can Transform the Way You Write," and her poetry can be found at the Academy of American Poets.

DAVID B. RAYMOND is a lifelong resident of northern New England and a student of Henry David Thoreau and his vision of good work. He has published a number of essays on Thoreau's philosophy of work. David is the chairman of the Arts and Sciences Department at Northern Maine Community College.

OWEN SHOLES taught biology and environmental science at Assumption College from 1978 to 2018. The author of several articles and *Stopping by Woods: Robert Frost as New England Naturalist*, he lives on five hectares in rural Massachusetts, where he cuts firewood, tends a vegetable garden, and observes the dynamics of the New England countryside with his wife, Claire.

WELFORD TAYLOR taught American literature at the University of Richmond, retiring in 2004 as James A. Bostwick Professor Emeritus of English. Among the works he has authored or edited on American literature and the graphic arts are Sherwood Anderson's *The Buck Fever Papers* (1971), *Amélie Rives (Princess Troubetzkoy)* (1973), *The Newsprint Mask* (1991), *Robert Frost and J. J. Lankes: Riders on Pegasus* (1996), *The Woodcut Art of J. J. Lankes* (1999), and *Sherwood Anderson Remembered* (2009).

MATTHEW TEOREY is a professor of English at Peninsula College. He is the author of *Self-Made Women in the 1920s United States: Literary Trailblazers* (2022).

HENRY WISE is an assistant professor of English at the Virginia Military Institute. A writer across multiple genres, his poetry has been published in *Shenandoah*, *Radar Poetry*, *Clackamas*, *Nixes Mate Review*, and elsewhere. His nonfiction has appeared in *Studies in American Culture* and *Southern Cultures*. His first novel, *Holy City*, about a crime in rural Virginia, is forthcoming from Grove Atlantic in June 2024.